Original Grace

Original Grace

The Mystery of Mary

Mary Aquin O'Neill, RSM

Foreword by
Margaret A. Farley, RSM

Preface by
Mary Rose Bumpus, RSM

CASCADE *Books* · Eugene, Oregon

ORIGINAL GRACE
The Mystery of Mary

Cascade Books
An Imprint of Wipf and Stock Publishers
199 W. 8th Ave., Suite 3
Eugene, OR 97401

www.wipfandstock.com

PAPERBACK ISBN: 978-1-6667-4442-2
HARDCOVER ISBN: 978-1-6667-4443-9
EBOOK ISBN: 978-1-6667-4444-6

Cataloguing-in-Publication data:

Names: O'Neill, Mary Aquin [author]. | Farley, Margaret A. [foreword writer] | Bumpus, Mary Rose [preface writer]

Title: Original grace : the mystery of Mary / by Mary Aquin O'Neill.

Description: Eugene, OR: Cascade Books, 2023 | Includes bibliographical references and index.

Identifiers: ISBN 978-1-6667-4442-2 (paperback) | ISBN 978-1-6667-4443-9 (hardcover) | ISBN 978-1-6667-4444-6 (ebook)

Subjects: LCSH: Mary, Blessed Virgin, Saint—Theology | Theology of the Blessed Virgin Mary | Feminist theology | Catholic Church—Doctrines

Classification: BT613 O54 2023 (paperback) | BT613 (ebook)

VERSION NUMBER 022223

Scripture readings are from The Holy Bible, containing *The Old and New Testaments with the Apocryphal/ Deuterocanonical Books. New Revised Standard Version.* New York: Oxford University Press, 1989.

Contents

Foreword

MARY AQUIN O'NEILL (1941–2016) has written a book for the ages. It has been written for those who yearn to know God, for those who yearn to understand human persons and their relationships, and for those who recognize that all real learning becomes love. Her book probes body and soul, night and day, here and now, and some of the ways to heaven and earth. It is alive in every way.

Her work was never, however, abstract. Her learnings came from her family, from studies in countless fields of learning, but also from her love of the Church, and even her choice to enter a religious community. Moreover, it came from her growing new understanding of feminism. But perhaps her learning was even more astonishing because it grew out of deep devotion to Mary as her Mother and the Mother of God.

This book unfolds in every chapter, and every chapter continues into the next. This does not mean that a chapter duplicates itself. It means that it brings something new as well as old. For example, scriptural foundations are key for O'Neill, but traditions are also sometimes lost because of differences in the interpretations of scriptural texts. It is within this book that O'Neill puts together her great work regarding our "Mary Our Mother." She grappled with ancient and modern texts regarding Mary, such as whether Mary was always subordinate to Jesus, or whether there could, in some way, have been an adult relationship between them. What might be between Mary and her Son, between Jesus and Mary when they both are together at the Cross?

The rise of consciousness among women in the twentieth century carried a hope for women's rights and goods, respect for the female body, for new ways for women to serve within the Church. But as O'Neill found, Catholic women were held back for some time because of theological strictures. As time has moved forward, the book has noted that Catholic women have grown in multiple ways in serving in the Church. But they, and we, have not gone far enough. No longer could women be simply inferior to men—in the family, in the world, in the Church. New ways, new patterns of relationships, began to open up. Women's experiences made sense to them, learning from Mary, her responses from God, her sharing of the Holy Spirit with Elizabeth, her asking her Son to bring wine that would give grace for those who needed it.

This book gives even more insight into the way O'Neill kept growing in her life in relationship to her beloved Mother of God. Between her knowledge of documents of the Church, and her literary approach to both history and narrative, O'Neill found much that made great sense over the years. This book has in it what the Church has long offered through the arts, music, painting—that was clear because it all fit! It is beautiful, and all the world can learn from Jesus, and Mary, and wonderful saints. All of this, was part of the life of Mary. And it offered O'Neill a way into the true depth of Mary's life for those who still live.

But O'Neill also worried that in our era there came a waning of women's deep devotion to Mary as their Mother and the Mother of God. It is true that many women were looking to find ways to know Mary as she, O'Neill, did. But some things were still missing. O'Neill brought original grace finally to the "paschal mystery." She brought with Mary the "cost of motherhood," the risks of her son in the temple, the people who derided her son, and even her son's followers when they abandoned him. Whatever was Mary's dark night, she came through it, as did her son. And thereby Mary also calls us in our time, and all women of all time, to follow her son, and bear both of them in their hearts.

But in all ways, Mary learned about God. This is why she knew that God was with her. And she gave to us, all women and sisters, our ways to know God, God's Son, God's Mother, God's children, our children, and our task of mothering and offering with new strength what can be in a renewed Church. The contents of this book have yielded what so many women (as well as men) have sought.

Margaret A. Farley, RSM

Preface

MARY AQUIN O'NEILL WAS born in Augusta, Georgia, on February 24, 1941, and was given the name Mary Ann. In her formative years she was taught by Sisters of Mercy and at age seventeen entered the Mercy community in Baltimore, Maryland. Shortly after entering, she received, and retained throughout her life, her religious name, Mary Aquin, after the great theologian Thomas Aquinas, a fitting name for her. Mary Aquin began her theological studies at the University of San Francisco (1967–70). She went on to earn an MA (1974) and a PhD (1981) in systematic theology from Vanderbilt University in Nashville, Tennessee. There she specialized in theological anthropology and feminist theory.

Mary Aquin spent her ministerial life as a creative and charismatic teacher, prolific lecturer and author, and a much sought after theologian. She was always interested in the deeper questions of theology as well as in the spiritual lives of her students. She served as assistant professor of theology at Loyola University Maryland before teaching at Salve Regina University, Rhode Island, and the University of Notre Dame, Indiana. She was a member of the Roman Catholic Southern Baptist Scholars Dialogue from 1986 to 1988, mentored students at the Ecumenical Institute in Tantur, Jerusalem, and lectured in the United States, Australia, and Argentina. In 1992, she returned to Baltimore where she co-founded with Diane Caplin, PhD, Mount Saint Agnes Theological Center for Women. Mary Aquin served as the guiding spirit of the Center until it closed in 2014; she then began to lecture and write full time.

Students of Mary Aquin reveled in her command of theology, her scholarly pursuits, her advocacy for women and the disenfranchised, and the respectful way she invited students to express their ideas or questions. They also took great delight in her Southern and biblical notion of hospitality. She believed that being called to the table of the Word meant being fed from the Scriptures as well as being fed from the kitchen. There she created many a delicious dish to enjoy in the midst of the community's theological pursuits. Mary Aquin was known by students and colleagues alike as a trailblazer for women in the Catholic Church. Early in her life she co-founded a task force on women within the Archdiocese of Baltimore. The task force prompted changes, including non-sexist language in the liturgy. Again and again, she sought to help women and others who felt marginalized or disenfranchised to explore their place in the Church and the world.

In all of this, Mary Aquin was highly influenced by her Catholic identity and her life as a Sister of Mercy. In 1991, at their first Institute Chapter, the Sisters of Mercy of the Americas committed their lives and resources to act in solidarity with the economically poor of the world, especially women and children, and with women seeking fullness of life and equality in Church and society. Ever committed to and shaped by the vision of the Sisters of Mercy, the Second Vatican Council, and her experience of women in the Church, Mary Aquin had been compelled to co-found Mount Saint Agnes Theological Center for Women. Those who participated in her courses and heard her lectures experienced the Center as a sanctuary and a place to belong—a safe place to explore the Scriptures and theology and to consider one's place in the Church and world.

When Mary Aquin left the Center and entered into a stage of full-time writing and lecturing, she began to see the relationship between her dedication to the advancement of women in the Church and in society and her devotion to Mary. She became convinced that there are images of Mary generated by the Christian imagination capable of liberating women from the kinds of theologies that privilege men over women. She also recognized that many women, since Vatican II, have limited their images and understandings of Mary only to those which can be delineated in the Scriptures. She believed this reduced the woman who served as the feminine face of God to a lesser role.

Mary Aquin wrote *Original Grace: The Mystery of Mary* out of her loving, living relationship with Mary as well as her vibrant, dedicated commitment to women. Through this work, she hoped to recover the tradition that imaged Mary as a woman who inspired and supported a sense of power and possibility for women.

Mary Aquin died unexpectedly on December 14, 2016, at age seventy-five. At the time of her death, she had been a Sister of Mercy for almost fifty-nine years and had shaped and influenced generations of women in relation to Church and society.

Many who highly value Mary Aquin's thoughtful and original reflections about Mary and her relationship to women and the Church believe she makes an invaluable theological contribution to the academic discourse on the role of Mary in the Church. She also offers the interested reader a way to be in relationship with a figure of Mary who empowers and inspires. We give thanks for Mary Aquin O'Neill's endeavor, and hope all readers will enjoy and benefit from *Original Grace: The Mystery of Mary.*

Mary Rose Bumpus, RSM

Acknowledgments

MARY AQUIN O'NEILL AND Wendy J. Hefter first met when Ms. Hefter was hired as a personal assistant to do several organizing projects at Mount Saint Agnes Theological Center for Women in Baltimore, co-founded by Mary Aquin and Diane Caplin, PhD, based upon a commitment of the Sisters of Mercy "to act in solidarity with women seeking fullness of life and equality in church and society." As O'Neill's workload permitted, she began sending Hefter the first few chapters of this book.

In 2014, when the Theological Center was about to close after twenty years, O'Neill and Hefter refocused their attention on packing up and moving O'Neill into her new home, shipping some archival materials to the Sisters of Mercy archives in North Carolina. Then, O'Neill was challenged by cancer for the second time, though she continued to work on this manuscript throughout her treatment.

Over the years, O'Neill and Hefter kept in touch through cards and emails. Hefter encouraged O'Neill to complete her book manuscript, some chapters of which had final touches in January 2016. However, although Mary Aquin O'Neill successfully beat the cancer, her body was too damaged from the chemotherapy to return to normal. She died on December 14, 2016.

Subsequently, Wendy Hefter told the Sisters of Mercy about her knowledge of the manuscript of *Original Grace: The Mystery of Mary.* The Sisters of Mercy of the Americas then engaged her to assemble from Mary Aquin's computer files O'Neill's last scholarly work. Thus, Wendy Hefter illustrates the beneficial collaboration of a generous, employed co-worker, who played an important role in assisting Mary Aquin O'Neill to address her goal, and for this we gratefully acknowledge and thank her.

We would also like to thank John R. Donahue, SJ, the Raymond E. Brown Distinguished Professor (Emeritus) of New Testament Studies at

St. Mary's Seminary and University, Baltimore, Maryland. He met Mary Aquin when he was teaching at Vanderbilt Divinity School where she was completing her doctoral studies. They kept in touch over the years, and Donahue, who knows and values Mary Aquin's work, faithfully helped in the publication of this book.

Finally, we would like to acknowledge the efforts of Mary C. Sullivan, RSM, without whom Mary Aquin's manuscript would not have found its way into the hands of you, the reader. Mary put the manuscript into its final form, persevered in searching for just the right publisher, and faithfully collaborated with all involved in the project. We thank Mary for the gifts she brought to this endeavor.

Introduction

MY MOTHER SAID THE rosary every night before going to sleep and whispered prayers to Mary during the day. If things were really bad, she also said the Seven Dolors rosary, which—to my regret—I never learned. For my mother, Mary was a familiar, a beloved figure who shared her life—both because Momma conversed with Mary, sharing whatever was on her mind, and because Mary was also a wife and mother. To my mother, Mary, this other Mary was always "the Blessed Virgin."

My father walked the vast expanse of the Savannah River Project (where the hydrogen bomb was built) with a string rosary in his pocket. He recited the prayers in between stops to supervise his men, who were constructing the plant. I cherish the memory of seeing him untangling his rosary before Mass, so that he could tell his "beads" (which were, appropriately for him, really knots) while the priest offered the holy sacrifice. For my father, Mary was the mother he never knew (his own having died in childbirth) and some sort of feminine ideal. He defended her like a knight of the Round Table when anti-Catholic literature about Mary circulated at his workplace. When he recovered from a surgery that almost took his life, he told us of having had a vision of the Blessed Mother, as he called her.

An oil painting of this beloved figure—Blessed Virgin, Blessed Mother—hung over my parents' bed for as long as I can remember. I spent a lot of time in my childhood trying to draw her.

I do not remember when I learned the Hail Mary or when it became the companion prayer to the Our Father. But it did. Throughout my youth, I participated in May processions, had May altars, learned the fifteen decades of the rosary, joined the Sodality of Mary, and wore her scapular. I always looked for her statue when entering a church and knew that, with Mary present, I was somehow represented in the holy of holies. This was important to me because, in the years I was growing up, a female could not function as an altar server or even enter the sanctuary except to clean it.

At the age of seventeen, I entered a religious congregation dedicated to Mary under the title of Our Lady of Mercy. There, I learned to say the Little Office of the Blessed Virgin Mary daily—first, chanted in Latin and, later, recited in English. The rosary was part of the religious habit worn by my congregation and each sister recited it daily. Together, we sang hymns to Mary, recited the litanies that praise her, and made novenas calling on her intercession. I grew to love Marian feasts, often celebrated with an abundance of flowers, the donning of church cloaks, and the opportunity to break the silence of our semi-cloistered lives at breakfast or after. Every sister had some form of the name of Mary as part of her religious name. Statues of her could be found throughout our convent homes, and images of Mary adorned many of the holy cards with which we marked our place in prayer books. Our rule of life inculcated devotion to her in these words:

> Devotion to the Mother of God has always been dear to religious persons. But as this Institute is immediately under her protection, and as the Mother of God is, under God, its principal Protectress, the Sisters shall nurture the warmest and most affectionate devotion to her, regarding her in a special manner as their Mother and the great model that they are obliged to imitate in order that, by her intercession and under her powerful protection, they may be enabled to fulfill the obligations proper to the Institute and to implant Jesus Christ in the hearts of the poor, whom they are charged to instruct.
>
> They shall have, individually, unlimited confidence in her. They shall have recourse to her in all their difficulties and spiritual wants; and, by the imitation of her virtues, they shall strive to render themselves worthy of her protection. They shall celebrate her festivals with joy and devotion and shall impress on the minds of all whom they can influence the greatest respect, veneration, and love for her.[1]

1. *Constitutions of the Institute of the Religious Sisters of Mercy of the Union in the United States of America* (1955), arts. 146–48. The current version of *Constitutions* has these lines: "Because Mary entered fully into her Son's mission she became the Mother of Mercy and our model of faith. Like Mary, we dispose ourselves to receive God's Word and to act upon it. This rhythm of contemplation and action is at the heart of our vocation to Mercy. Devotion to Mary, the Mother of God, prompts us to honor her in both prayer and action. In Mary's *Magnificat*, mysteries of the Rosary and other devotions, we find sources of reflection and renewal for our life and ministry." *Constitutions and Directory, Sisters of Mercy*, arts. 15, 15.1.

When I made my vows "until death," it was "In the name of our Lord and Savior, Jesus Christ, and under the protection of His Immaculate Mother, Mary ever Virgin."

Graduate studies in the time after the Second Vatican Council posed real challenges to this devotional life. Scripture scholars, under the influence of the historical-critical method, considered the texts that spoke of Mary less historically reliable than other texts. So much about her occurs, after all, in what came to be known as "the infancy narratives." I don't remember any Catholic scholars daring to say that the foundational stories about her were "myths," but the clear insinuation was that no one serious about the intellectual life could invest much faith in them. For the professors who were Protestant, the issue was not even engaged, for there was not the same tradition of Mariology to contend with or about which to be concerned.

Many theologians seemed by and large embarrassed by the Mariology that had developed over the centuries. Seen now in the light of the new ecumenism, the claims made for Mary looked to them extravagant and were to be explained away, defended against. I clearly remember a beloved Jesuit professor exclaiming that, when it came to Mary, some of the best scholars seemed to lose their heads. Need it be said that the scholars referred to were male? Women were at that time only beginning to study theology seriously, and few had written books. Vatican II had placed the liturgical and theological emphasis on Jesus the Christ. One of the most heated debates of the Council was over how to deal with Mary in the documents produced by that body. In a very close vote, the decision was made not to dedicate a separate document to Mary, but to include her in *Lumen Gentium: The Dogmatic Constitution on the Church*. The final chapter of that document is entitled, "The Role of the Blessed Virgin Mary, Mother of God, in the Mystery of Christ and the Church." In addition, those who were endorsing new titles for Mary (e.g., Mediatrix of All Graces) lost out. The presence of Protestant observers at the Council surely placed such claims for Mary in a negative light. The only new title given to her came from Pope Paul VI without the advice or consent, much less the vote, of the council fathers. Pope Paul declared her "Mother of the Church."

The stress placed on liturgical prayer after the Council exerted an influence on the ideal of prayer in religious life. Though no one said our devotions should go by the board, it was in the air that "praying with the Church" meant the Divine Office, not the Little Office of the Blessed Virgin

Mary; it meant meditating on the texts used at Eucharistic liturgy, not on the mysteries of the Rosary, for example. Gradually, and in ways that I cannot reconstruct, devotion to Mary diminished in my own congregation. The rosary was no longer said at the wakes of our sisters; the Feast of Our Lady of Mercy became "Mercy Day"; we changed the office to a shortened form of the Divine Office; sisters no longer bore the name of Mary as part of their individual name, for baptismal names were allowed and, I would say, promoted. With the change to a modified habit, the rosary was no longer worn on the person. Dropping the requirement to have Mary as part of the religious name, and the subsequent move to "secular" dress, removed the last vestiges of communal external displays of devotion to Mary. Some individuals might wear a medal or carry a rosary, but it was out of private devotion, not community observance.

The rising feminist consciousness in the decades after the Second Vatican Council led to a re-examination of the ideals presented to Catholic women and, with them, of devotion to Mary. Whether one was wife or mother, single person or woman religious, Catholic women had been socialized to the ideal of the "hidden life" (often associated with Mary's life at Nazareth). This meant being content to have our efforts go unnoticed, being the helpmate of the men in our lives, striving to be humble, self-effacing, pure, and a bulwark of traditional morality. Above all, it meant accepting that women's roles would always be subordinate to those of men.[2]

Though the brilliant Mary Daly saw clearly the lineaments of the great goddess preserved in the powers attributed to Mary by her devotees, she also wrote that women "are enslaved symbolically in the cult of the virgin Mary, who is glorified only insofar as she accepts the subordinate role assigned to her."[3] Gradually, many feminists became suspicious of the way in which devotion to Mary has been inculcated by the men of the Church, finding in this devotion a way to "ambush women's aspirations to personhood, human dignity, and co-responsibility for the church and society," in the words of Patricia Noone.[4]

In this atmosphere of academic suspicion of anything not capable of passing the test of historical criticism, and of feminist disdain for traditional

2. Read quotes a friend of hers who said of Read's fascination with Mary: "I don't get it; she's such a drip." Read understands that "Mary symbolized everything we liberated women were supposed to reject: modesty, chastity, submission." See Read, "My Poetic Path to the Virgin," 10.

3. Daly, *The Church and the Second Sex*, 61.

4. Cited in Johnson, "The Tradition and the Reality of Women," 120.

Marian piety, I learned to keep quiet. It reminds me now of an incident from my childhood. When I was little, there was a young woman who worked in our house (surrounded, I might note, by images of the one we called the Virgin Mary). Probably because my mother had been talking with her about Catholicism, this young woman once beckoned me into the pantry to say, "I don't care what you say, Miss Mary Ann, that Mary was fooling around with some man." I never told a soul that that happened—until now. Somehow, I knew it was (a) not disrespectful on her part and (b) not to be understood in my household. Best be quiet, as we say in the south!

Years passed. I wrote papers on everything but Mary in graduate school, and, as a result, I did not think of her as often. It seemed that my relationship with her belonged to a former life. When I tried to think about her in my new role as theology student, everything I thought seemed so childish. I had no way to defend or explain my love for her or the sources of my love for her.

A dissertation on Paul Ricoeur's work on the imagination began the recovery.[5] This was followed by several years of teaching undergraduates, during which time I came to know William Lynch's work, especially the brilliant *Images of Faith*.[6] The death of my mother brought me to a new stage. In a burst of energy and insight, she made herself known—my mother and Mary. Suddenly, I began to see connections and to read Scripture with other eyes. Now an associate professor of theology, I still shied away from writing what I was thinking for publication. But, in private, I began to realize how related are my devotion to Mary and my dedication to the advancement of women in the Church and in society.

Especially through teaching in the area of theological anthropology, I saw a disturbing pattern. Both creation myths of Genesis include a female as well as a male, and women interpreters have successfully challenged any notion that the inferiority of the woman is written into the text. Likewise, responsibility for the expulsion from the Garden, and all that the Garden means, is shared equally by the man and the woman, according to current interpretations. Yet, when it comes to the story of redemption, Christianity posits a lone male redeemer. He is born of a woman and has women disciples, but in the theology of redemption developed by male theologians subsequent to the New Testament witness, Jesus has no female counterpart and all women in the story are subordinate to him. It is no wonder, then,

5. O'Neill, "Revealing Imagination: A Study of Paul Ricoeur."
6. Lynch, *Images of Faith.*

that it has been impossible for Christianity to view women as equal to men and co-responsible for the Church's mission, despite a theology of sanctification that brooks no difference between men and women.

A favorite author illustrates the difficulty. William Lynch, writing of the "new irony" introduced by the Christian revelation, has this to say:

> To work out a new irony is a difficult and never-ending task. In the centuries since Christ, it had to and did lead to a complete democratization of the image of man and to the impossibility of any theology built upon class or race or nation; all these categories were destroyed by this overwhelming idea of men as sons of God.[7]

Great as he is, Lynch seems not to have noticed that this "democratization of the image of man" leaves intact a theology built upon sex; that the "idea of men as sons of God" excludes half the human race.

What Christianity needs, it seems to me, are images that can destroy any theology that privileges one sex over another. I am convinced that there are images of Mary generated by the graced Christian imagination that are capable of such a liberating effect. The effort of this work will be to show this to be true.

Doubtless, the master narrative about Mary, developed by male theologians in times and cultures convinced of the inferiority, if not the curse, of women, reflects biases that need to be challenged. As one who believes firmly in the possibility of revelation, I maintain that those deformations of the scriptural texts and of the subsequent tradition do not exhaust their meanings. In fact, I believe that new possibilities for women in the Catholic Church go hand in hand with an understanding of Mary purified of sexism and renewed in power.

Devotion to Mary

This book is being written, then, out of devotion to Mary and a commitment to women. I realize that devotion is an old-fashioned term, not much in use today. In fact, I was reminded of that fact when a young mother whom I know asked me what it means to have devotion to someone or something. Let me make a foray into this mysterious realm.

To have devotion to someone is, first of all, to have a loving relationship with that person. By relationship, I mean something living, present,

7. Lynch, *Images of Faith*, 100.

daily—or, at least, regular—and influential. It means that one shares important moments with that other, that one creates or participates in rituals of contact, of conversation, of remembrance, of celebration. For instance, a friend of mine told me that long ago she gave her mother a statue of Mary kneeling (which went by the name of "*adsum,*" meaning "here I am"). For the remainder of her life, her mother began the day by patting the statue on the head and saying, "Mary, this is what I would like you to do today." Here you can see a familiar, daily, loving, and important relationship, on which her mother counts for assistance.

Or in a very different vein, those of us who watched the coverage of the fortieth anniversary of D-Day saw an original act of devotion (even if all did not recognize it as such). An American veteran who had made the trip to the Normandy beaches cemetery, knelt down, took an envelope from his pocket, and said, as he poured the contents over a grave, "You're gonna get a little dirt from where you were born, kid." What worlds of feeling led to that simple and eloquent gesture we will never know.[8]

Note in each of these cases the direct address. We are not dealing with someone remembered as a figure from the past, but someone who can be addressed in the moment. This is a living relationship. Though the example of the veteran involved a one-time act, you can be sure that he thought about what he would do for many months prior to going and that he thinks about those who gave their lives with great regularity. Such a symbolic act of reverence could arise from nothing less.

"Having devotion," then, requires some sacrifice—of time, energy, resources, attention. We could not say we are devoted to mother or family or Church or even a sport if we never spend time with the object of devotion. Of course, by terming devotion "a loving relationship," I have already intimated sacrifice, for what love can be without it? A final note on this question comes from Robert Orsi: "Devotionalism is the space where the body, otherwise denied, insists on itself in Catholic cultures. . . . Devotionalism is the embodiment of desire and . . . prayer is desire's search for a voice with which to speak."[9]

When I say that this is a book written out of devotion to Mary, I mean several things. First, it arises from a relationship with her that is integral to

---

8. At the funeral of Senator Ted Kennedy, one of those eulogizing him referred to what Senator Kennedy took to the funeral of Itzak Rabin, who had been assassinated: soil from the graves of the Senator's slain brothers, John and Robert.

9. Orsi, "She Came, She Saw, She Conquered."

my life. I cannot remember a time when I did not know and love her. Oh, I can remember times when I neglected her, as I did my natural mother, but no matter my neglect, I never doubted that she was reaching out to me.[10] Second, I seek to honor Mary by writing this book. I intend it as an act of fealty. Third, I write in the hope of helping others discover her and have devotion to her, especially women who have been confused by versions of Marian piety and theology. I want to help others relate to Mary as a living person, not as a memory—dangerous or otherwise.[11] Finally, I intend to base some of my argument on what Catholics call "devotions," those rituals that have become part of the Catholic heritage.[12] They reflect the loving relationship that Catholics have had with Mary and the manifold ways we have perceived and imagined her. It is my hope that this work can inspire new "devotions," so that our age will contribute to that great stream of prayer and praise to this glorious daughter of God.

The rising of women in the twentieth century remains, in the twenty-first, the most important "sign of the times" for me and, I think, for the Church whose daughter I am. Despite the progress that has been made in theological anthropology—progress that has eliminated from Catholic teaching convictions about the inferiority of women—there is still a terrible imbalance in the life and teaching of the Church where women and men are concerned. I do not think this situation can be rectified until and unless we get our thinking about Mary straightened out. In my opinion, this will require letting go of some cherished notions and opening ourselves to a paradigm shift of great proportions. In the process, we might be reminded that the development of doctrine is not over.[13] Moreover, we might

10. Wells captures this sense beautifully in lines from *Divine Secrets of the Ya Ya Sisterhood*: "Sidda stands in the moonlight and lets the Blessed Mother love every hair on her six-year-old head. Tenderness flows down from the moon and up from the earth. For one fleeting, luminous moment, Sidda Walker knows there has never been a time when she has not been loved." Cited in Baker and Budde, *A Sourcebook about Mary*, 102.

11. "Dangerous memory" is a phrase that is frequently in use in feminist circles. Johnson repeatedly applies it to her work on Mary (see *Truly Our Sister*). In my opinion, this emphasis risks reducing Mary to a historical figure whom we remember (and whose memory can inspire us), but not someone with whom we can have a vital relationship in the present tense.

12. As noted, devotions always involve bodies. Orsi is quoted to that effect by another author: "Devotionalism was the site at which Catholic bodies and architecture, the material and the spiritual, imagination and reality, hope and resignation came together." Cited in Mitchell, *The Mystery of the Rosary*, 222.

13. Ryan reminds readers of this in "Orthodoxy & Dissent," 17: "The church,

feel some of the excitement earlier ages knew when forging a theological consensus.

It is equally important that, by defending the Catholic devotion to Mary, I might make a contribution to the devotional life of our separated sisters and brothers. They certainly defended their devotion to the Word of God, and in the process brought Catholics back to reading the Scriptures as an approved and regular part of our prayer life. As I have experienced and studied Protestant Christianity, it is poorer for having lost the living presence of Mary. Or perhaps I should say, for having lost a tradition of reflection on the presence of Mary.

My doctoral studies were done at Vanderbilt in Nashville, Tennessee. Vanderbilt is now non-sectarian, but has a strong Methodist tradition arising from past affiliation with that denomination. As a Catholic sister, I was something of an exotic in this setting, and was often asked to speak to Protestant women's groups. Regardless of the topic, before the night was out at least one woman in the crowd would seek a chance to tell me that she prays to Mary. Often her "confession" was prefaced by "Don't tell my preacher, but . . . ." My mother, who was a great informal evangelizer (though she would not recognize herself in that description), talked with women wherever she went—selling Avon, selling insurance, selling real estate. She, too, knew that many Protestant women longed for a womanly figure of ultimate holiness in their lives of prayer and devotion.[14] Protestant women often talked with my Catholic mother about her devotion to Mary.

Years later, when I served on a Scholars Dialogue between Roman Catholics and Southern Baptists, I strongly advocated that the group visit the Shrine of the Immaculate Conception while meeting once in Washington, DC. Despite objections from several Catholics in the dialogue, we did so. As was to be expected, reactions were varied, and the discussion afterwards was lively and illuminating. One Baptist scholar was taken with a quote inscribed over a side chapel in honor of Our Lady: "To Jesus through Mary." In his ruminations about the quote, this staunch Baptist believer said, "It makes me wonder if one can go to Jesus without Mary." It

---

individually and collectively, is forever *docens et discens,* teaching and learning. To deny the possibility of further elucidation of doctrine is blasphemous. It is tantamount to pronouncing the church dead, no longer vivified by the Spirit nor tending toward an ultimate manifestation still to come, when all that has been hidden will be revealed."

14. For a most interesting account of a Protestant mother and daughter who have discovered the power and significance of devotion to Mary, see Kidd and Taylor, *Traveling with Pomegranates.*

was another indication to me that our reluctance to claim and explain our devotion to Mary has short-changed our ecumenical partners.

Of course, in some instances what is encountered is the fear of the feminine that permeates Christianity. In that case, it becomes important to define oneself by a determinedly male set of images for the holy. In other words, *not* having devotion to Mary is a defining element of Protestant identity for many—including women—even if they have no idea why it is forbidden to do so. There are some signs that this is changing. Witness the number of books and articles on Mary in Protestant publications of late, though the authors are usually careful to keep her in the past, as some kind of exemplar.[15] It is still too Catholic to consider her a living presence to whom one can address concerns and from whom one can seek assistance.[16]

Missing Mary

My own story illustrates, I believe, the trajectory for many women in the years since Vatican II. Eager to "think with the Church," we followed the path of those whom Charlene Spretnak identifies as "Catholic progressives." They are convinced that "the radical shrinkage of Mary to strictly biblical delineations" is a necessary step to modernizing the Church and making possible more fruitful ecumenical discussion.[17] Elizabeth A. Johnson's work, *Truly Our Sister*, is a good example of the theology that emerges from such shrinkage. There, Mary is above all a Nazarene woman, whose life differed little from the other women of her time. Mary is a woman of the Spirit, sometimes even a prophet, but in no way does Johnson want her to function as a transcendent symbol. Mary remains a disciple and is never crowned Queen of heaven and earth, as celebrated by the liturgy. Mary is someone to identify with, if one is poor and oppressed, but not a woman of power to whom one would bring petitions for assistance. Having rejected what she calls the "patronage" model of sanctity, both here and in her book on the communion of saints, Johnson eschews the age-old tradition of calling on Mary and the saints for protection, assistance, or deliverance.

15. For example, see Donahey, "Mary, Mirror of Justice," 71–87; Yeago, "The Presence of Mary," 58–79.

16. Spretnak quotes an Episcopal divinity student as saying: "There's still a great deal of wariness in our church about acquiring *any* Mariology . . . and *praying* to the Virgin Mary is extremely unappealing, pretty much unthinkable." See *Missing Mary*, 87.

17. Spretnak, *Missing Mary*, 1.

This tamed and blanched version of Mary's story has failed to inspire anything like the great hymns, prayers, and works of art fueled by the more imaginative and traditional images of a cosmic Mary, a heavenly Mother. Charlene Spretnak raises a host of important questions relative to this reduction of Mary:

> Has the diminution of the bounteously compassionate Mother of God really improved the Catholic experience? Has the "rationalizing" and narrowing of the sacramental presence in Catholicism been a boon? Are Catholic women better off spiritually now that Mary has been deposed from her cosmological throne and made their strictly human sister? Did Catholic men benefit from her grand maternal presence as the Mother of the Church in their formative years and beyond?[18]

In my opinion, women are not only worse off spiritually, but we are weakened in our position in the Church, having lost an important foundation for an argument for equality. The move that Vatican II made away from what is called the "christo-typical" approach to Mary, with the consequent enshrining of the "ecclesio-typical" approach, has had, in my opinion, a negative effect on the status of women as a whole as far as the Church is concerned. Once it was possible to see the mystery of the Christ reflected in female form through the person and imagery of Mary. This made it at least possible that all women could be considered capable of imaging the Christ. The recent Mariological emphasis, however, has been on associating Mary with the Church, which, as the "body," is always subject to the "head." Inasmuch as the hierarchy are also associated with the "head" and the laity with the "body," this subordination is extended to all those who are not ordained in the Church. No matter how much praise is heaped on Mary, the lines of *Lumen Gentium* relegate her and all she does to a subordinate status:

> Embracing God's saving will with a full heart and impeded by no sin, she devoted herself totally, as a handmaid of the Lord, to the person and work of her Son. In subordination to Him and along with Him, by the grace of the almighty God she served the mystery of redemption . . . .
> The Church does not hesitate to profess this *subordinate* role of Mary.

18. Spretnak, *Missing Mary*, 10.

She experiences it continuously and commends it to the hearts of the faithful, so that encouraged by this maternal help they may more closely adhere to the Mediator and Redeemer.[19]

Later on, I will have more to say on about what I take to be the inordinate attention to Protestant objections to the Catholic tradition on Mary. The resulting theology has had the effect of reducing a figure who once functioned as the feminine face of God to near insignificance. Witness the virtual disappearance of rituals honoring Mary in churches that have attempted to renew according to Vatican II.

Over the years, having watched thinking women turn to forms of goddess worship or to an exaltation of Mary Magdalene, I can only conclude that they are in search of female figures that inspire and sustain a sense of power and possibility for women. I seek to recover the tradition that imaged Mary as chief among them for women.

Tracing a Developing Tradition

Since the close of the New Testament, stories about Mary have expanded the narrative of her life. Feast days, liturgical texts, and private devotions limn an understanding of her that goes far beyond what can be known from the four evangelists. Beloved of artists, Mary appears in images painted and sculpted; lines about her inform literary efforts from sophisticated poetry to humble hymnody. Two significant modern dogmatic declarations on the part of the Catholic Church confirm her sinlessness and her presence, body and soul, in the heavenly realm.

I will trace the contributions of such works of the imagination to the growing tradition about Mary. It will also be necessary to analyze efforts to contain and/or redirect that development and the subsequent effects of those efforts on the position of women in the Church.

Throughout this book I will face into the winds of the full feminist critique of the Marian tradition. The complaints against Mary have traditionally centered on the understanding of virginity as key to her holiness; an exaltation of the role of mother as incumbent on all women; and an exclusive identification of Mary with the passive or receptive side of human activity. I will argue that a post-critical understanding of Mary's virginity, her divine motherhood, and her stance as a "summoned subject" is not

19. Abbott, Vatican Council II, *The Conciliar and Post Conciliar Documents: Lumen Gentium*, arts. 56 and 62. Emphasis added.

only possible but essential to the advancement of women in the Christian churches. I will also show that the images of Jesus and Mary accepted by the liturgical tradition imply a complementarity between them. Perhaps, in the end, a theology of complementarity will be more advantageous for women of the Catholic Church than the current theology of headship that requires male leadership and an unrelenting identification of women with the laity who make up the body of the Church. I believe there is a distinct possibility.

The Productive Imagination

To understand the approach taken here, it is necessary to know a bit about the imagination—what it is and how it functions in the life of faith and in theology, which is a disciplined reflection on that faith. The first chapter, therefore, lays down a foundation for understanding the connections among imagination, faith, and experience. I am in quest of a more embodied theology, one that admits symbols and images to the exalted space long held by ideas alone.

To accomplish this embodied theology, which is especially important with respect to Mary, I must clear away some misunderstandings. The first concerns misleading images of faith, the most important of which for my purpose here is that faith is separate and distinct from experience. Following William Lynch, I will maintain that faith is a way of experiencing the world. As such, it is shaped by what happens to real human beings in time and space. This gives faith a body, a history, and means it is inseparable from human experience.

At the same time, I must clear away some misunderstanding of the imagination itself. In the popular mind, to imagine is to "make things up." But for Lynch, the task of imagination is "to imagine the real."[20] This puts imagination in the realm of reality and truth, not fantasy. Though Lynch worked in a very different arena from Paul Ricoeur, there are interesting points of contact. One of the most important concerns the determination to rescue the imagination from its reputation as fanciful or unreal.

Ricoeur has made an important distinction between the reproductive and the productive imagination. It is the productive imagination that works, through metaphor, to re-describe reality and to affect the way one sees things and, potentially, to change the way one acts in the world one sees. It is the mysterious power to "see one thing as another" that is at the

20. Lynch, *Images of Faith*, 63.

heart of metaphor and, I will argue, at the heart of understanding the Marian tradition, beginning with Scripture and continuing up to the dogmatic declarations of the immaculate conception and the assumption.

Disentangling the Marian Tradition

In a post-critical world, in the world of the "second naiveté," it is imperative that religious thinkers discontinue mixing the worlds of historical truth, biological or scientific truth, and theological truth. Ricoeur has argued that a mix of biological and theological truth accounts for the difficulties that plague the doctrine of original sin.[21] I will argue that the same applies to the doctrine of the virgin birth. This will require a daring acceptance of the real nature of the sources for this belief and a mature understanding of what the doctrine means in the life of faith.

At the same time, it is necessary to admit that no interpretation represents the only possible way to understand, when one is dealing with works of the imagination. At the core of the great "seeing as" that is metaphor lies the power to convey multiple meanings at once—what Ricoeur calls a "surplus of meaning." In the history of faith, meanings emerge and submerge, often in conjunction with the experience of the people. One must be on guard against using (consciously or unconsciously) one's own time and concerns as a Procrustean bed, ruling out interpretations of meaning that have sustained the life of faith of previous generations. Yet, at the same time, it is possible to conclude that some interpretations are death-dealing. The Catholic community has recognized this with respect to the portrayal of Jews in the New Testament and in much preaching based on it heretofore. It is not so widely recognized how destructive certain interpretations of the Marian tradition have been for women and for the laity in general in the Catholic Church.

A correlative task, then, is to search out some criteria for evaluating interpretations of Scripture and of tradition. The Church that presents herself as a pilgrim needs to stand ready to correct what has been injurious to her daughters, even as she has already done with respect to separated brothers in the Christian community and elder brothers in Judaism.

---

21. See Atkins, "Paul Ricoeur (1913–2005).

CHAPTER 1

Yearning for the Divine Feminine

Introduction

THE RISE OF CONSCIOUSNESS among women in the twentieth century was accompanied by a concomitant rise in longing for a representation of the divine feminine. Women sought to learn about the tradition of goddesses; joined groups that devised rituals honoring female existence, especially the female body; turned in some cases to reverencing witches and attempting to relearn their ancient customs and cures. Throughout the second half of the twentieth century and into the twenty-first, books poured out, offering resources in these areas as their subject matter. As Janine Canan observed, the titles read "like a crescendoing chant."[1]

One would think that Catholic women, in possession of the rich Marian tradition, would have had something to contribute to this search for a female divine image. We were held back, however, not only by theological strictures against associating Mary with God, but also by feminist critiques of the figure of Mary based on a number of accounts. Elizabeth Johnson gathered a selection of these criticisms in her 1985 article on "The Marian Tradition." She references the following: Patricia Noone called Mary a "Trojan horse," designed to "ambush women's aspirations for personhood, human dignity, and co-responsibility"; Mary Daly charged that "women are enslaved symbolically" by devotion to a Mary who "accepts the subordinate role assigned to her"; Kari Børresen wrote that it is absurd "to make

---

1. Canan, ed., *She Rises Like the Sun*, xxi.

Mary the model for free women" as long as this link between femininity
and subordination is unbroken; and, Marina Warner indicted Mariology as
a "weapon in the armory of male chauvinism."[2]

Johnson herself offers three trenchant critiques in that same article.
The Marian tradition, she contends, has been "associated with the deni-
gration of the nature of women as a group"; has "dichotomized the being
and roles of women and men" in the churches; and has "truncated the
ideal of feminine fulfillment and wholeness."[3] In line with the last point,
Johnson disparages the exaltation of Mary's virginity if it means that the
"highest peak of the history of female sexuality is its non-use."[4] As women
came to claim the goodness of sexuality in general and our own sexuality
in particular, this negative attitude toward Mary, occasioned by the traditional interpretation of her virginity, gained momentum. It is notable that
many Catholic women cultivated a devotion to Mary Magdalene, not only
because she was "the apostle to the apostles" who exercised leadership in
the early Church, but also because of what was taken to be her passionate
nature and her intensely human love of Jesus the Christ.

Still, there were some women—such as the daring Mary Daly—who
saw that the Marian tradition is infused with the power and the attraction
of the goddess. Early depictions of Jesus Christ drew on the artistic representations of Apollo, the beardless boy-god. In time, painting and statues
of Mary likewise borrowed and adapted conventional images of Isis, the
Egyptian goddess who is often shown holding her son, Horus. According
to cultural historian, Charlene Spretnak, numerous symbols of the goddess
were transferred to Marian imagery, among them birds (especially the dove)
and the moon.[5] Though the associations have slipped from consciousness,
it is undeniable that the Christian imagination and its works preserve an
ancient memory, if not desire, for a female representation of the sacred.

The Undocumented Virgin

I borrow this marvelous phrase from Rubén Martínez, who applies it to the
Virgin of Guadalupe.[6] For my purposes, however, it serves to capture the

2. Johnson, "The Marian Tradition," 120.

3. Johnson, "The Marian Tradition," 121–29

4. Johnson, "The Marian Tradition," 127.

5. Spretnak, *Missing Mary*, 183–84.

6. Martínez, "The Undocumented Virgin," in Castillo, *Goddess of the Americas*,
98–112.

insights about Mary that have not been officially approved, yet live in the experiences of her devotees and in the stories they tell of her. Unencumbered by a dogmatic tradition that puts limits on what can be thought and written, these seekers after the divine feminine have discovered in Marian art a power to inspire awe, and in the figure of Mother Mary, an enduring source of consolation in the midst of woe. Some, such as China Galland, were once Catholic and left the fold because of upset over the symbolic exclusion of women in Catholic ritual life. Others, like Sue Monk Kidd, come from the Protestant tradition, whose prohibitions against devotion to Mary left women without a primary female figure in their religious imaginations. Still others, like Eliza Gilkyson, profess no religious commitment, yet find that Mary is the one to whom they turn when devastating events occur. At least one of these women, Clarissa Pinkola Estés, remains Catholic and has found in her ethnic roots the courage to write of Mary in ways that counter the debilitating fear of the goddess that marks much of Catholic writing. These women conjure up a Mary who is sovereign, self-contained, endlessly concerned for all who are poor and suffering, and a partner to her son in the redemption of the world.

China Galland finds words for an experience several women of my acquaintance have had. When hearing certain phrases used at Mass—such as "Our Father," "His Body," "His Blood," and "Glory be to the Father"—she says that she feels smaller and smaller, "as though something in the room is suffocating me." When Mass is over, the tears come forth, as she relates how she had come home to the Catholic Church after a long time away "only to find that [she is] a stranger."[7] She became a student of Buddhism, in which practice she came to know about Tara, a female Buddha. The discovery of an enlightened one who has a body like her own sent Galland on a search to learn more about this figure. It was on this journey that she met, time and again, an image of Mary as the Black Madonna, an image that challenged her to exceed the limits of her own interiorized restrictions about associating Mary with God. After seeing one of these representations, she writes:

> Seeing the Madonna at Einsiedeln [Switzerland] gives me the sense that she is a Western remnant of the ancient Dark God . . . .
>
> I use the word "God" fully intending to draw on the resonance and power that such a term can carry in Western culture. The word "goddess" connotes a mythological time past rather than actual present time. It tends to allow one to dismiss this manifestation of

7. Galland, *Longing for Darkness*, 14–15.

God as little more than a concern of feminist scholars and a vestige of a lost and sometimes hypothetical past.[8]

Galland is not writing as a theologian here, but rather as a woman searching for a female image of the sacred. She is determined that Mary be liberated from the Catholic Church, for Mary, she writes, "belongs to everyone who longs for a richer, more vital conception of a power greater than ourselves, which some choose to call God."[9] In language abounding in evocation, Galland calls Mary, "a taproot that reaches to the center of the earth and a root system that stretches around the globe."[10]

Sue Monk Kidd, in whose best-selling novel, *The Secret Life of Bees*, a statue of Mary plays a central part, recounts in a subsequent book her developing relationship with Mary. The encounter was particularly mysterious since Kidd was raised Baptist and had all of the Protestant negative instincts where Mary was concerned. An unusually self-aware person, Kidd realized that she needed an image in order to carry on a relationship with the divine. While traveling in Greece, she remembers a "crude little icon" that a stranger had given her at a book signing.[11] This memory prompts an interest, which leads her to seek out icons of Mary. Despite her misgivings as a feminist and a Protestant ("Just a woman; just a woman," she chants to herself regarding Mary), something in her can't let it go.[12] She records experiences with Mary in her journal and comes to a hunch about why this figure has become so important:

> If I penetrate to the center of Mary's image, perhaps I will find a
> new center of myself. Isn't that what iconic images are meant to
> do: bring us into encounters with our own deep selves? My heart
> and my gut tell me that the night-skinned, fierce-eyed, tree-loving
> Mary will help lead me to the inner sanctum of the Old Woman;
> that she has something to do with my rebirth as an older women.
> I can't explain this to myself.[13]

On one of her trips when accompanied by her daughter Ann, Kidd is shocked by the younger woman's openness to Mary. After an awkward and

8. Galland, *Longing for Darkness*, 158.

9. Galland, *Longing for Darkness*, 159.

10. Galland, *Longing for Darkness*, 161.

11. Kidd and Taylor, *Traveling with Pomegranates*, 45.

12. Kidd and Taylor, *Traveling with Pomegranates*, 47.

13. Kidd and Taylor, *Traveling with Pomegranates*, 53.

extended attempt to explain her "Mary" problem, Kidd hears her daughter saying, "All I know is if Mary wants to be the feminine face of God for you, why don't you just let her?"[14] Perhaps prompted by Ann's simple yet startling question, Kidd gradually resolves the conflicts she had been experiencing relative to Mary and begins to see her as "a spiritual presence able to hold large archetypal mysteries."[15] She even begins to relate the events of Mary's life to those of her own and to find in them enigmatic depths.

Toward the end of her book and her travels, Kidd returns to a Marian site that had deeply impressed her. At Palianis Nunnery on her first trip to Greece, Kidd had met *Panagia Myrtidiotissa* (Virgin of the Myrtle Tree). It is a large, glass-plated icon to be found in a myrtle tree. Legend holds that each time those who found the icon carried her into the church, Mary escaped back to the myrtle tree. Finally, they gave up and left her there, "like a tomboy returned to her true element," Kidd comments.[16] When Kidd was found staring at the icon, she was told by one of the nuns to ask the Virgin for something and, when she grants it, to give something back to Mary. It was the mission of giving something to the Virgin that prompted Kidd's return to the place, where she offered a small jar of South Carolina honey: an item that plays a central role in the novel she successfully completed after asking the Virgin for her help. These words conclude her search for the divine feminine and her embrace of Mary: "I know she is not a figure in a tree or in a church, but a presence inside. She is a way to meet the divinity in myself."[17] Now, Kidd freely avows that Mary is "the primary icon of devotion" in her life and her muse,[18] which is quite an admission for a Protestant feminist.

Shortly after the March 2011 tsunami in Japan, National Public Radio interviewed singer and songwriter Eliza Gilkyson. Gilkyson is not Catholic, yet she composed and sang a haunting hymn to Mary, asking her to sustain those who are suffering. When the interviewer asked why she turned to Mary, Gilkyson responded:

14. Kidd and Taylor, *Traveling with Pomegranates*, 98.

15. Kidd and Taylor, *Traveling with Pomegranates*, 147.

16. Kidd and Taylor, *Traveling with Pomegranates*, 52. It is notable that, in the appearance of Mary at Beauraing, Belgium, she came down from the sky to stand before a hawthorn tree.

17. Kidd and Taylor, *Traveling with Pomegranates*, 255.

18. Kidd and Taylor, *Traveling with Pomegranates*, 281.

> Mary is such a strong, compassionate icon, one of the strongest
> female archetypes we have today. . . . I researched all types of fe-
> male archetypes, Muslim, Buddhist, and so on, and I kept coming
> back to Mary.

Her hymn overflowed with images of a woman who can rescue in the face of overwhelming tragedy. Something in this woman draws poets and releases in them a flood of fresh images that reveal the enduring power and mystery of Mary.

No one whom I have read is more passionate or more poetic with regard to Mary than Clarissa Pinkola Estés. A lifelong devotee of Our Lady of Guadalupe, Estés writes of her in ways that encourage ordinary individuals, especially those living on the mean streets of ghettos and barrios, to relate to this transcendent figure. From her official website, we learn the following about Estés: She is an American poet, psychoanalyst, and post-trauma specialist. Due to her heritage, which is Mestiza Latina, this author is acquainted with nearly-vanished oral and ethnic traditions upon which she draws in her writings. Among her many ministries are service to injured and "castaway" children, women who have lost children, and male and female prisoners. All of this informs what Estés has to say about Guadalupe.

The essay, "Guadalupe: The Path of the Broken Heart," illustrates her style. Writing to correspondents who are inquiring about *La Sociedad de Nuestra Senora de Guadalupe*, Estés describes what she calls "visits" from Our Lady:

> She appears in times that are not calm, in clouds of dust that are
> not particularly picturesque. She comes skidding to a sudden stop
> in dark cars on even darker gravel roads. She stands in the midst
> of broken glass at curbs. She walks in every street, stands at every
> street corner, even those where it seems that maybe even God
> Herself ought to be cautious.[19]

In the same essay, she blithely re-describes "virgin" in terms that might speak to the young: "brilliantly colored, fierce, watchful, with the loyalty of a good dog."[20] Her most daring depiction of Guadalupe in this essay comes at the end, however, where Estés, quoting from her own sixty-five-page poem, *"Mi Guadalupe,"* describes Mary, not as an unmoved and unmoving woman dressed in blue, her hands joined in prayer, but as the

---

19. Estés, "Guadalupe: The Path of the Broken Heart," 35.
20. Estés, "Guadalupe: The Path of the Broken Heart," 39.

vigorous young leader of a gang in heaven, moving with ample, sturdy hips like an ocean or a sunrise.[21]

A subsequent, book-length work, *Untie the Strong Woman*, continues the reimagining of Mary, or perhaps I should say the work of freeing her images so that they can help us reimagine ourselves. Estés writes:

> She wears a thousand names, thousands of skin tones, thousands of costumes to represent her being patroness of deserts, mountains, stars, streams, and oceans. If there are more than six billion people on earth, thereby she comes to us in literally billions of images. Yet, at her center is only one great Immaculate Heart.[22]

The author is determined to counter those who would "pare down the numinous," making Mary "an appendage to a group of historical facts."[23] Here one finds a living relationship with a powerful transcendent figure, a relationship that allows the devotee to call upon the might of Mary to help those who are themselves tied down, oppressed by life's trials, or undergoing great suffering. Chapter 11 is a good example. There, the author recounts her successful efforts, with the help of Mary, to have some of the girl inmates to whom she taught poetry abandon their "mother fucker" tattoos for words more empowering of their womanhood. It is quite a narrative.[24]

To read Clarissa Pinkola Estés is to be immersed in a world of rituals, prayers, poems, and images that put one in touch with the mystical tradition of Marian devotion. It is a world that too often comes in for scorn at the hands of those trained in the rational traditions of Catholic theology. Yet, it is a realm young people in particular seek in other ways, having been deprived of it in their own Christian upbringing.[25]

Though there are other examples of this more liberated approach to imagining Mary, one more will suffice here. It is from the prize-winning novelist Zadie Smith. In her work, *NW: A Novel,* a pregnant thirty-something inhabitant of London encounters Mary in a medieval church in Willesden. The marvel of the following passage is the way Mary throws challenges at her:

21. Estés, "Guadalupe: The Path of the Broken Heart," 45.

22. Estés, *Untie the Strong Woman*, 2.

23. Estés, *Untie the Strong Woman*, 18–19.

24. Estés, *Untie the Strong Woman*, chapter 11.

25. When I taught in college in the 1980s, students were playing records backwards and dabbling in the occult, all in an effort, in my estimation, to access something mysterious.

How have you lived your whole life in these streets and never known me? How long did you think you could avoid me? What made you think you were exempt? Don't you know that I have been here as long as people have cried out for help? Hear me: I am not like those mealy-mouthed pale Madonnas, those simpering virgins! I am older than this place! Older even than the faith that takes my name in vain! Spirit of these beech woods and phone boxes, hedgerows and lampposts, freshwater springs and tube stations, ancient yews and one-stop shops, grazing land and 3D multiplexes. Unruly England of the real life, the animal life! Of the old church, of the new, of a time before churches. Are you feeling hot? Is it all too much? Did you hope for something else? Was there more to it than that? Or less?[26]

All of these passages reveal a contemporary search for a female figure of strength and power to whom modern women can relate in an intimacy that, in turn, empowers.

Mary in the Documents of the Church

If, on the other hand, one turns to the official documents of the Catholic Church regarding Mary, what depictions of her emerge? Is there anything to answer the yearning of highly conscious women for the divine feminine? A review of representative documents exposes a move in quite the opposite direction. It is important to note that all of these documents are written by men and reflect an outside point of view on Mary as woman. Despite the fact that the writings concern the foremost woman of the Catholic Church, none of them cites the work of women.[27]

Chapter 8 of *Lumen Gentium: The Dogmatic Constitution on the Church* of Vatican II presents the official teaching of the Catholic Church on "The Blessed Virgin Mary, Mother of God in the Mystery of Christ and the Church."[28] In this document, each time Mary is extolled there is a sentence or phrase to temper that acclaim and to remind the reader that she

26. Smith, *NW: A Novel*, 83.

27. A curious dimension of the first Encyclical of Pope Francis, *Laudato Si'*, is that despite the innovation of using sex-inclusive language, there is not a single citation of a woman author, even though the fact is that women have written with authority on the topic of the environment.

28. Trouve, "Dogmatic Constitution on the Church, *Lumen Gentium*, Chapter VIII," in *Mother of Christ*, 73–82. This is Trouve's own translation of *Lumen Gentium*.

is, in all ways, subordinate to and in no way a competitor for her son. Thus, while Mary is called "Mediatrix," a term that would mean she has the power to intercede for her devotees and to channel divine power, the text reiterates that Christ is the one Mediator.

Though Mary is acknowledged as Mother of God, a title that would seem to hold authority, the text declares that "she devoted herself totally as a handmaid of the Lord to the person and work of her Son, under him and with him" (#56). This notion is repeated in stronger terms when the Council Fathers proclaim, "The Church does not hesitate to profess this subordinate role of Mary" (#62). For women seeking a model of partnership with men in Church and society, the Vatican II document—replete as it is with praise for this singular woman—undercuts the potential for finding that model in Mary. The move to ensure that all understand Mary's subordination to her son culminates in the titles given to her by popes and biblical scholars since the Council; for example, "Mother of the Church" and "first disciple." Again, the former title should convey a position of prominence and of leadership, but is diminished by the latter, which ignores the realities of motherhood and of alternate interpretations of important biblical texts, and sees her as one who—in all ways—follows the lead of her son. Certainly, what these titles convey in the official documents is a far cry from the engaging images of the "undocumented virgin."

Pope Paul VI was aware that some traditional images of Mary were turning women away from her and from the Church. His effort in the Apostolic Exhortation, *Marialis Cultus*, is to emphasize Mary's "active and responsible consent" and her "courageous choice," which the Pope believed would speak to the modern women of his time.[29] This image of self-direction is quickly undermined, however, by the Pope's insistence that Mary "offers them the perfect model of the disciple of the Lord" (#37).[30] There is a lovely passage toward the end of the document that asserts: "It is impossible to honor her, who is 'full of grace' (Lk 1:28), without thereby honoring in oneself the state of grace." How can women identify with this idea, however, when an ensuing sentence teaches that devotion to the Blessed Virgin is "a powerful aid for man as he strives for fulfillment" (#57)? This insistence on sex-exclusive language, a usage about which "modern women" have

---

29. Trouve, "For the Right Ordering and Development of Devotion," in *Mother of Christ*, 158.

30. I consider this a loss because she who was once known as "Queen of the Apostles" has been reduced to a follower of her son, disregarding the ways in which she led him and, later, led the burgeoning Christian community.

complained for decades, endures until the time of Pope Francis, he being the first pope to write in an inclusive manner.

No pope of recent history has been more public about his devotion to Mary than John Paul II. His papal motto, *"Totus Tuus,"* proclaimed that he was totally hers. He dedicated the bullet that pierced his body to Our Lady of Fatima, whom he credited with his survival. He wrote several extended meditations on her and regularly referred to Mary in prayers and in exhortations. There is one stunning passage in *Redemptoris Mater* (Mother of the Redeemer) in which he observes that, in certain icons, "the Virgin shines as the image of divine beauty, the abode of Eternal Wisdom, the figure of the one who prays, the prototype of contemplation, the image of glory" (#33).[31] Here, John Paul II comes close to seeing in Mary the divine feminine. Nevertheless, later paragraphs evince the same determination to underline her subordinate position (e.g., #39 and #41).

This pope, too, seems somewhat conscious of Mary's meaning for women. But is it at odds with what he wrote in his first encyclical: *Redemptor hominis* (Redeemer of Man)?[32] There, he asserted that "Christ the redeemer 'fully reveals man to himself'" (#10). Presumably, this use of "man" is intended to include woman. Yet in *Redemptoris Mater*, he claims that "the figure of Mary of Nazareth sheds light on womanhood as such" (#46), implying, it would seem, that Christ the redeemer does not suffice where women are concerned. That there should be need of special attention to women in a Church where all are to be conformed to Christ Jesus raises questions about what anthropology is at work here. The same problem occurs in his lengthy work *Mulieris Dignitatem* (On the Dignity and Vocation of Women), where John Paul II states that Mary is "the full revelation of all that is included in the biblical word 'woman': a revelation commensurate with the mystery of redemption."[33] In a later chapter, I will consider reasons for this seeming nervousness about considering Mary to have the power of Mediatrix and the difficulties with the claim that Jesus the Christ reveals "woman to herself" (a legitimate alternative version if "man" includes woman).

Pope Benedict XVI was more reserved in his writings about Mary, always emphasizing her role as archetype of the Church. In his sole monograph on her, *Daughter Zion*, originally published in 1977 before he became

31. Trouve, "Mother of the Redeemer," in *Mother of Christ*, 287.

32. John Paul II, *"Redemptor hominis,"* 631.

33. Trouve, "On the Dignity and Vocation of Women," in *Mother of Christ*, 395.

pope, Cardinal Joseph Ratzinger avoids all talk of Mary as "Mediatrix," considering her instead in the light of a typological interpretation of the Old and New Testaments. By this, he means an exegesis that sees "the cohesion of the one history in many histories."[34] The resulting portrait of Mary says little of her historical reality and treats her mainly as "the beginning and the personal concreteness of the Church."[35] Statements made about Mary during the time of his papacy do no more to offer justification for women seeking an image of the divine feminine in Mary, the Mother of God. The official documents of the Church continue to insist on the subordination of Mary to her son and the inferiority of her contribution to God's work of salvation, a stance that is problematic for women as we seek grounds to confirm a call to partnership in Church and society.

Mary Reconsidered in the Light of Feminism

The challenge for feminist theologians is to remain within the Catholic tradition while avoiding the interpretations of Mary that have contributed to the disempowerment of women. Among the problematic interpretations are those that image Mary as totally passive, exceptional rather than representative in her privileges, and holy because of her physical virginity. In addition, feminists with a certain kind of ecumenical consciousness also want to avoid any exaltation of Mary that would put her in rivalry with Jesus.

I do not intend to review all works on Mary by contemporary feminist theologians, but I do want to select a representative to show the trend in modern Mariology among theologians with a feminist consciousness.[36] The leading thinker in this arena is clearly Elizabeth A. Johnson, whose work has exerted a wide influence. For some time, Johnson has been opposed to considering Mary "the feminine face of God." In fact, she thinks that many of the extraordinary feminine qualities attributed to Mary rightly belong to God and should "travel back" there.[37] She is especially insistent that the association of Mary with wisdom be discontinued. In addition, Johnson objects to what she calls "the patronage model" of relationship between

---

34. Ratzinger, *Daughter Zion*, 32.

35. Ratzinger, *Daughter Zion*, 67–68.

36. Maeckelberghe has reviewed quite a few versions in *Desperately Seeking Mary*, 3–39. However, the book is necessarily somewhat out of date.

37. See Johnson, *Truly Our Sister*, 73.

saints in heaven and the faithful on earth.[38] By that, she means the model that regards the faithful as dependent on the intercession of those who are considered friends of God. In this company, she includes Mary. To that end, Johnson's 2003 book, *Truly Our Sister*, was subtitled *A Theology of Mary in the Communion of Saints*.

In characteristic fashion, Johnson exhaustively reviews other attempts at a Marian theology. In each case, she shows what she considers to be the deficit in that approach and its meaning for women.[39] The author is especially critical of any approach that depends on a dualistic anthropology, wherein women and men have separate and definable roles based on gender.

Having rejected, as what she calls "cul-de-sacs," the roads that consider Mary the ideal face of woman or the maternal face of God, Johnson begins her search for "a way forward" with a statement of her "modest proposal." It is "to locate [Mary] in the communion of saints and there to remember her, dangerously and consolingly, as a woman with her own particular history among her contemporaries and before God."[40] This emphasis on "remembering" and on recreating Mary as an historical personage will eventually undermine the vital relationship between believers and Mary as she now lives, according to Catholic teaching, in the entirety of her personhood (body and soul) with God, reigning with Christ in glory.

In the central portion of one of her works, which is so popular that it has been separately published, Johnson offers her own reading of scriptural passages where Mary appears, developing her theology of Mary almost exclusively from this reading.[41] She corrects a passive image of Mary by emphasizing Mary's prophetic role, especially in the glorious song known as the Magnificat. There, Johnson hears "a protest against the suppression of women's voices and a spark for their prophetic speech," making Mary a representative of all that women can be when called by God.[42] In a somewhat surprising line, Johnson claims that, to Mary, "the call has come to partner God in the great work of redemption."[43] Curiously, she seems to

---

38. Johnson, *Friends of God and Prophets*, 86–92.

39. Johnson, *Truly Our Sister*, chapters 3 and 4.

40. Johnson, *Truly Our Sister*, 95.

41. See Johnson, *Dangerous Memories*.

42. Johnson, *Truly Our Sister*, 263.

43. Johnson, *Truly Our Sister*, 265.

see no contradiction between this assertion and another repeated image of Mary as the first disciple of her son.[44]

Johnson walks a very careful line when approaching the question of Mary's virginity. While not denying the belief, she nevertheless interprets the marriage of Mary and Joseph as tempering the problematic dimensions of the virgin. Writing on Luke 2:21–40 where the parents together present the child, she muses:

> in a church tradition that has long ignored Mary's married status in favor of an idealized portrait of the virgin mother and, more to the point, has used that image to relegate married women to subordinate status, it is surely liberating to give Mary back her marriage, to give her back her relationship with the man with whom she shared her life, for better or worse. And to know that this is blessed.[45]

At this point, Johnson does not engage the traditional belief that the marriage of Mary and Joseph was without sexual union, both before and after the birth of the Christ Child. This is one of the contemporary stumbling blocks to considering their marriage as paradigmatic for Christian couples.

Johnson's hermeneutic of Mary in Scripture begins and ends with the prior assumption that Mary is a disciple of her son. Despite passages that highlight Mary's independent action in the story of the annunciation, her role as prophet in singing the Magnificat, and the initiative that, in effect, influences her son at the wedding feast at Cana, Mary remains for Johnson a follower of her son, not a woman whose mission is given by God, to whom she is accountable. Moreover, the exemplary virtues displayed by Mary in Johnson's interpretation of the Gospel passages do not seem to carry over into Christian history beyond the Scripture. Mary is a memory, not a presence.

In the end, the Mary who emerges from Johnson's book is an admirable Jewish peasant woman of the first century, with whose life journey, when properly considered, women can identify, but who seems—if I read Johnson correctly—to have little power to assist any who invoke her name.[46] She encourages "those still running the race," but does not intercede.[47] Mary

44. Johnson, *Truly Our Sister*, 247 and 255.

45. Johnson, *Truly Our Sister*, 282.

46. Athans also seeks to find "the real Mary," with an emphasis on her Jewishness, in her work, *In Quest of the Jewish Mary*.

47. Johnson, *Truly Our Sister*, 313.

does not receive accolades because, "rather than praising her, we join with her in praising God."[48] This beloved figure functions no longer as archetype, symbol, or in any other transcendent fashion. She is St. Mary or, as Johnson writes, "one such paradigmatic figure" in the communion of saints.[49] "The narrative of her life can teach, inspire, and cheer on the lives of the people of God today."[50] For those longing for the divine feminine or for a womanly personage to connect with in a circuit of saving grace, Mary as cheerleader will hardly appeal. In addition, though Johnson writes fluently of "the still-developing egalitarian anthropology of partnership," no such partnership appears here between Mary and her son.[51]

One obstacle to mutuality between Mary and Jesus is Johnson's preference for the ecclesiotypical hermeneutic of Mary rather than the Christotypical. What this means is that Mary is interpreted as a "special member of the community of the church," in whom one can see the destiny of the *ecclesia*.[52] This preference leads Johnson to abandon any attempt to see a parallel between Mary and Jesus, as the Christotypical approach does. Furthermore, in identifying Mary with the Church, she reinforces the subordination that exists between the Church, his body, and Christ the head. In privileging the ecclesiotypical interpretation, Johnson is following the lead of Vatican II and its highly contested decision to include what was said about Mary in the document on the Church. Though the author is capable of criticizing other aspects of the Vatican II document, this path is clearly convincing for her, despite its drawbacks.[53]

The theological struggles here seem clear and mark other versions of Marian theology written by feminists. Desirous of an "egalitarian partnership" between women and men in the Church, we are faced with a doctrinal tradition that insists on Mary's subordination to Jesus in being and in mission. The association of Mary with the Church only serves to underscore this subordination not only of women, but of all the laity. Mary's position on the "pedestal," where male theologians have firmly placed her, makes her—in the words of Marina Warner—"alone of all her sex." Authors who thus drastically reduce Mary's position leave us with an historical Mary who

48. Johnson, *Truly Our Sister*, 324.

49. Johnson, *Truly Our Sister*, 313.

50. Johnson, *Truly Our Sister*, 314.

51. Johnson, *Truly Our Sister*, 53.

52. Johnson, *Truly Our Sister*, 125.

53. Johnson, *Truly Our Sister*, 66.

has no power beyond being a model for discipleship, which others are as well. Moreover, what was once the cosmic presence of a woman who reigns with God becomes the memory of one who once lived but now serves only as an example. The significance of the two Marian dogmas, the immaculate conception and the assumption, has been blunted if not erased.

Charlene Spretnak is one thinker who has taken exception to any move to unseat Mary from her throne and diminish her heavenly powers. Her book, *Missing Mary*, is a sustained theological argument for the one whom she calls "big Mary" or "grand Mary"—Mary the "Maternal Matrix," who is Advocate, Mediator, and Intercessor.[54] Spretnak sets her face firmly against the ravages of modernity on the riches of Marian devotion when she writes:

> Regarding the argument that contemporary women can "relate" to Mary only if she is shrunken down to the proportions of a socially committed Nazarene woman, one sees here another pitfall in the reductionist ideology of modernity: the narrow modern focus on the individual self at the expense of realizing the larger context in which individuals exist. Modernity reduces the ineffable to its own proportions rather than stretching to meet, even partially, the boundless mystery of life with symbol and metaphor. It makes sense to think of Mary as a human "companion" only if one refrains from slipping into the mechanistic understanding of what a human is: As Mary walked the streets of Nazareth, as she did the daily work of a wife and mother, as she observed the practices of Jewish worship, she was also a cosmological being, one linked—as are we all—with every other manifestation of the universe, one held in the gravitational embrace, one constituted from one nanosecond to the next by the unimaginable range of subtle relationships that form and inform a living entity.[55]

I intend to take up this challenge and read the Marian tradition in such a way that it stretches us to "meet, even partially, the boundless mystery of life with symbol and metaphor." In particular, I search for grounds to see in Mary's relationship with God an evolution toward partnership with Jesus the Christ, in which she becomes one in whom the union of humanity and divinity reveals the divine feminine. A search of this kind necessarily relies on the grace of the imagination which, by the inspiration of the Holy Spirit, has been a guide for the development of dogma. My search is motivated by

54. Spretnak, *Missing Mary*, 76.
55. Spretnak, *Missing Mary*, 76–77.

an intuition that as long as Mary is considered subordinate and her contributions to the history of salvation understood as inferior to those of her son, there is no chance for true mutuality or reciprocity for women and men, lay and ordained, in the Church. Along the way, the objections of the theologically orthodox to a hermeneutics of partnership and the critiques of the thoughtfully feminist to the misuses of the Marian tradition will be confronted.

The Way of *Approfondissement*

It will not be possible to proceed in a linear fashion when considering the scriptural texts, images generated by devotions, and dogmas related to Mary. Rather, I will go by a path learned from the French poet, Charles Péguy. Anyone who has read his poetry knows that Péguy works and reworks a theme, returning each time with a more profound expression. It is called *approfondissement,* a French expression meaning a process of continually going deeper into the meaning of a reality.

CHAPTER 2

Scriptural Foundations
of the Marian Tradition

Introduction

ANYONE WHO APPROACHES THE question of Mary in the Bible faces what amounts to a tradition produced by the work of generations of historical critics. That tradition is clearly seen in a work like *Mary in the New Testament*, a volume resulting from the Lutheran/Catholic Dialogue and based on conversations among scholars steeped in the historical-critical method.[1] Their goal is to drive backward as far as possible toward the "historical Mary" by considering each relevant text in the setting in which it appears. *Mary in the New Testament* thus exemplifies the method of historical criticism. It considers each of the New Testament texts on its own, beginning with the most primitive or earliest writings of Paul and continuing through the four Gospels to the book of Revelation.

The Picture of Mary Arising
from Historical-Critical Research

The most extensive information about Mary in the New Testament comes from the Four Gospels, and the text under consideration, *Mary in the New Testament*, concentrates on them. Mark, as the presumptive first Gospel

---

1. Brown et al., *Mary in the New Testament.*

written, is given initial consideration. Though Mary only appears in one scene here, the text in which she is included exercises considerable influence over subsequent interpretations. The passage in question is Mark 3:31–35:

> Then his mother and his brothers came; and standing outside, they sent to him and called him. A crowd was sitting around him; and they said to him, "Your mother and your brothers and sisters are outside, asking for you." And he replied, "Who are my mother and my brothers?" And looking at those who sat around him, he said, "Here are my mother and my brothers! Whoever does the will of God is my brother and sister and mother."[2]

For historical critics, this is a privileged passage, for it has parallels in Matt 12:46–50 and Luke 8:19–21. Such parallels make it more likely that the passage has some historical validity. When the authors of *Mary in the New Testament* come to interpret this and the similar passage in each of the other two Gospels, the lesson drawn is that Jesus is determined to replace the family of the flesh with an eschatological family, which the family of the flesh is eligible to join on the conditions that Jesus has laid down. Their supposition is, however, that the family (including the mother) does not understand Jesus and is not—at the moment—within the circle of Jesus' new community. Moreover, though subsequent Synoptic versions tone down what the scholars take to be Jesus' criticism of his family, the authors' commitment to the Markan rendering affects their interpretation of several significantly different texts, as I will show.

The image of Mary that emerges from the ecumenical work on Matthew's Gospel is Mary as "an instrument of God's providence in the messianic plan."[3] Since Matthew shines the spotlight on Joseph in his account of Jesus' conception and birth, and the mother plays no role in Jesus' public ministry, there is little to be said of the character of Mary. Considering her an "instrument" renders her a passive tool in the hands of God.

Luke's Gospel, on the other hand, is replete with narratives in which Mary stars or has a prominent role: the conception and birth of Jesus, the visit to Elizabeth, the presentation of the infant Jesus in the temple, and the finding of the child in the temple. The scholars of *Mary in the New Testament* draw from these texts the conclusion that Luke is presenting Mary as the first to hear the gospel and thus, as the first Christian disciple. By

2. Mark 3:31–35.

3. Brown et al., *Mary in the New Testament*, 82–83.

associating her also with the "Poor Ones," of the Psalms, Luke thus "gives her "an important role in . . . salvation history, a representative role that will continue from the infancy narrative into the ministry of Jesus and finally into the early church."[4] Still, the question of the status of her motherhood lingers. These authors interpret the "sword" that Simeon prophesies will pierce her soul[5] as referring to "the difficult process of learning that obedience to the word of God transcends family ties."[6] Again, in the episode of the finding of the child in the temple, their emphasis falls on the same theme: that Jesus (who is assumed to be, even at twelve, superior in knowledge to his parents) must place his relationship with the heavenly Father ahead of any ties to Mary and Joseph. The lovely and repeated phrase used by Luke, whereby Mary "treasured all these things in her heart,"[7] is taken to mean that she continued to search for an understanding that escaped her at the time.[8]

The study of Luke concludes with a consideration of the lines in the book of Acts where Mary is included among those who are in the Jerusalem upper room, "constantly devoting themselves to prayer."[9] The authors confess that this passage was, for them, "somewhat unexpected," since Luke makes no mention of Mary at the crucifixion scene.[10] They surmise that this final mention of Mary shows her "of one accord with those who would constitute the nascent church at Pentecost."[11]

There are only two occasions on which Mary appears in the Gospel of John: the wedding feast of Cana and the crucifixion. In the first instance,[12] the authors of *Mary in the New Testament* interpret Mary in the scene as misunderstanding Jesus, perhaps because she thinks of him as a wonderworker. In other words, she is asking him to misuse his powers. They interpret the question that Jesus poses to Mary when she points out the lack of wine—"Woman, what concern is that to you and to me?"—as an indication

---

4. Brown et al., *Mary in the New Testament*, 143.

5. Luke 2:35.

6. Brown et al., *Mary in the New Testament*, 157.

7. Luke 2:19 and 2:51.

8. Brown et al., *Mary in the New Testament*, 162.

9. Luke 1:14.

10. Brown et al., *Mary in the New Testament*, 173.

11. Brown et al., *Mary in the New Testament*, 177.

12. John 2:1–14.

that what Mary asks for is not within the scope of his vision of his mission.[13] The subsequent statement—"My hour has not yet come"[14]—they see as evidence of Jesus' dissociation from his mother's interest. The narrative gives them no little trouble, however, since Jesus *does* act on what they take to be Mary's implied request. If Jesus did not understand himself as commissioned to intervene in a wedding, and if he was convinced that his "hour" had not yet come, then what accounts for this turn in the story? Of all the passages in this study, this one most clearly demonstrates the control that the conclusions drawn on the basis of Mark 3:31–35 have for the interpretation of narratives written later. The scholars insist that in Jesus' words to his mother, "We are very close to the Synoptic tradition wherein Jesus contrasted the claims of an earthly family with the will of God."[15]

When it comes to the scene under the cross,[16] the scholars understand John as bringing Mary "into the context of discipleship": something that, according to them, was not the case at the wedding feast.[17] They assume that Jesus' words to John mean that John is to take care of the mother. They drive home once more that the primary symbolism here is "based on a new eschatological family relationship to Jesus stemming from discipleship."[18]

The work of these historical critics as they interpret the New Testament texts results in a minimalist picture of Mary. Her role as mother is of little value since what counts, in their opinion, is discipleship, by which they seem to mean following Jesus and heeding his teachings. Moreover, her son knows more than she does at every stage of his development: an assumption that severely undercuts the role of parenting in the life of Christ. Similarly, the image of Mary as an "instrument" of God undercuts any sense of her agency. All suggestions that the new creation theme that opens the Gospel of John means that Mary can be seen as the new Eve are discounted by the majority as not within the evangelist's intention.[19] Mary is reduced to a minor character in the New Testament, who in no way advances or affects the narrative. Rather, she is used by God, corrected by her son, excluded from the circle of disciples, and eventually given into the

13. Brown et al., *Mary in the New Testament*, 191.

14. John 2:4.

15. Brown et al., *Mary in the New Testament*, 192.

16. John 19:25–27.

17. Brown et al., *Mary in the New Testament*, 206.

18. Brown et al., *Mary in the New Testament*, 218.

19. Brown et al., *Mary in the New Testament*, 190.

care of the beloved disciple where, according to the Fourth Gospel, she is finally endowed with spiritual motherhood and "meets the criterion of the eschatological family."[20]

The Catholic Tradition on Mary

The foregoing picture contrasts sharply with the Catholic tradition where Mary is concerned. If one were to ask, "How do we know what we know about Mary," the Catholic answer would be a complicated one. Certainly, the framework and foundation are supplied by the stories in the New Testament where she appears or is discussed. But these passages are surprisingly few, given the knowledge of her that Catholics claim. The New Testament does not speak of her birth, but there is a feast day—complete with liturgical texts—that does, as well as icons and other works of art that depict it. There is no mention of her being presented in the temple, but the same holds true for that. Scripture does not provide an account of how her life ended, but Catholics know that Mary's destiny was to be with God: body and soul. Her whole self was taken up for that purpose. Moreover, another feast indicates that she has been given a crown comparable to that of Jesus and that she reigns with him over "heaven and earth."

That she was a virgin when she gave birth to Jesus is documented in the New Testament, a fact rarely disputed by anyone who reads the text. On the other hand, the perpetual virginal character of that motherhood and the sinless nature of her being are far from clear to those who rely on Scripture alone. Still, Catholics are assured of it. Equally confident are we that she met her son on his way to crucifixion and that he appeared to her after the resurrection, though, except for John's Gospel, all the New Testament indicates is that she was with others in the upper room as they prayed together after the ascension of Jesus.[21]

We have counted the number of her joys and her sorrows and celebrated a round of feast days that, together, fill out the gaps in what is known from Scripture alone, so we are not surprised when stories of her appearances surface. When a pope claims that Mary saved his life when he was seriously wounded by a gunshot,[22] it is not cause for protest among Catholics.

20. Brown et al., *Mary in the New Testament*, 213.
21. Acts 1:12–14.
22. Meissen, "A Mother's Hand Guided the Bullets."

Such an expanded narrative, one that far surpasses what can be known from Scripture alone, raises questions about the sources and validity of such knowledge about Mary.

A Literary Approach

I readily acknowledge that the tradition about Mary just described, as well as the devotion to her, developed (and will continue to develop) in large measure due to what I will call "the graced imagination" of Christian believers. After all, most of what we know of her story from the New Testament appears in texts that are "one of a kind"; that is, not corroborated in other Gospels. Prime among the examples are the infancy narratives: texts that most scholars now consider a type of "inspired fiction."[23] Other aspects of her story are culled from the Protoevangelium of St. James, an apocryphal work whose historicity is questionable at best. Still other episodes have been generated by private devotions such as the Stations of the Cross and by public devotions enshrined in liturgical feasts. The artistic tradition has perpetuated many of these extra-testamental stories through icons, paintings, sculptures, hymns, and poems.

For those committed to the historical-critical method, such an admission would be reason enough to dismiss this tradition as unreliable. Current trends in hermeneutics, however, make possible a different approach to the Marian tradition. This fresh approach admits its own reliance on the imagination, yet it also defends such reliance on the basis of the significant "world" opened up for women and men in an age that suffers from the absence of the divine feminine. In other words, there is an argument for legitimate revelation in the expanded Marian tradition.

It is unquestionable that any claim about revelation must be based on Sacred Scripture.

At issue is the method by which the many meanings in those sacred texts can be realized and validly interpreted. The historical-critical method—which analyzes texts with a view to establishing the historical validity of an interpretation based on what the text meant at the time it was written, as well as on the history of its composition—yields a certain kind of information about biblical texts. This method aims at getting "behind" the text to the intention of the author and to the meaning contemporary hearers or readers would have derived from the text. In the many years since the

23. Brown refers to the infancy narratives as "inspired fiction," a correlative term.

publication of *Mary in the New Testament,* new approaches to the study of Sacred Scripture have emerged. Scholars have recognized that, as Sandra Schneiders writes, "It is intrinsic to the nature of literature to be polyvalent rather than univocal in its meaning and therefore to call forth different interpretations from different people at different times."[24] St. Gregory the Great expressed it more simply, "Scripture grows with its readers." That means that the intention of the author and the meaning a text had in its original context cannot control the meanings that come to light at the hands of new interpreters.

In addition, there is a growing awareness that the Bible is the book shaped by—and, in turn, shaping—a community. The value of the texts is not primarily in their historical accuracy but in the power of their testimony. It is my contention that the Gospels testify to an evolution in the life of Jesus, in the life of the community, and in the consciousness of his followers.[25]

The literary or poetic approach to texts of Sacred Scripture attempts to reveal the world "before" the text, the world that is opened up when believers approach the text with contemporary insights and arrive at heretofore unrealized aspects of the text.[26] That revelation requires another approach: one that works not only with the whole individual text, but with the entire tradition. The approach of which I speak allows one to "dream" over texts and lets the mind make connections back and forth among them. Here, all texts are contemporaneous. In a sense, nothing is past, but everything is present to the reader. Because of this, not only can a previous text influence the interpretation of a later one, but the reverse can occur.[27]

In one sense, the method under consideration is a return to an ancient approach to the biblical texts, one familiar to the fathers of the Church and medieval exegetes. In another sense, it is new, since the consciousness of the interpreter must now be post-critical; that is, in the language of Paul

---

24. Schneiders, "Faith, Hermeneutics and the Literal Sense of Scripture," 722.

25. Brown has traced the evolution in the life of the Johannine community, but his work and the work of others of his kind seem to presume that there is little or no change in Jesus himself.

26. For an analysis of the way in which the search for the "literal sense" has morphed, see Schneiders, "Faith, Hermeneutics and the Literal Sense of Scripture," 719–36; Guite, *Faith, Hope and Poetry,* 28. For a comprehensive review of changes in biblical interpretation, see Donahue, "Things Old and Things New," 20–31; and Donahue, "The Literary Turn and New Testament Theology," 250–75.

27. See the very interesting work of Hayes, *Reading Backwards: Figural Christology.*

Ricoeur, it must involve a second naiveté.[28] A post-critical consciousness requires full awareness that the biblical texts cannot and do not yield the same kind of information found in modern historical and scientific writings. The second naiveté allows a person to admit this and, at the same time, read the texts for a meaning that transcends what history and science can apprehend or express.

An ancient approach that, combined with a post-critical consciousness, generates insights into spiritual meaning in biblical texts is *lectio divina*. This prayerful way of reading biblical texts requires a kind of "mastication which releases in full flavor."[29] Urging that poetry be read this way, literary critic Malcolm Guite maintains that the first fruit of this slower savoring of the text will be a new openness to the powers of echo and counterpoint, of the tension between the words themselves and the way the words of a poem speak to each other across the lines.[30]

Guite goes on to show how the images evoked by words and phrases also partake of this interplay, not just in a single poem but across "the whole interrelated network of poetry that is our inheritance." To illustrate, Guite shows how one of T. S. Eliot's lines in *The Waste Land* echoes and is reshaped by one of Dante's in the *Inferno*. The echo ties the two works together in such a way that the mind can begin to glimpse a similarity between the London rush-hour crowds and the souls in limbo who just drifted through life. Guite makes the strong claim that, in a profound sense, "After Eliot, Dante's poem is changed forever." Moreover, he argues that the influence is mutual: "Each poem subtly modifies all the poems with which it is connected, running backwards and forwards through time across the great web of Poetry itself."[31]

This way of reading, which allows the mind to dream over texts and meditate on words, symbols, and narratives, permits the reader to apprehend connections that open up new depths of meaning. Texts can be "dreamt" about if they contain what Paul Ricoeur calls a "surplus of

28. See Leclercq, *The Love of Learning and the Desire for God,* as cited in Guite, *Faith, Hope and Poetry,* 26. See also Peterson, *Eat This Book.*

29. Guite, *Faith, Hope and Poetry,* 27. In *Reading Backwards,* Hayes also speaks of the importance of "echoes."

30. Guite, *Faith, Hope and Poetry,* 28.

31. Guite, *Faith, Hope and Poetry,* 29. The artist, too, can accomplish this collapse of time. Dupré notes "this de-centering of the present moment" and says that "the effect is to dissolve the perception of the specific, historical moment and release the viewer into *Kairos,* or ahistorical divine time." See *Full of Grace: Encountering Mary,* 75.

meaning." This richness results from using language in a poetic fashion that employs words, phrases, and images to convey multiple meanings. Such an employ contrasts with the scientific use of language whereby the intention is to control language and make it serve a singular purpose by tying down its meaning to a singular significance.

An example might help. When Shakespeare has Cleopatra remember the time when she was "green in judgment," he is clearly not speaking scientifically.[32] Judgment has no color. The only way to understand what Shakespeare is saying is to relinquish the literal meaning and search for something connoted by "green" that will fit the term "judgment." Under the musing of the mind, several possible meanings come up: young, tender, naïve, full of life. They all fit, and Shakespeare does not tell us which of them, if any, he intends. Nor would it matter if he did, for the meaning is in the making for poetry, not in the intention of the author.[33] That is, poetic language is not controlled by the poet's intentions. Once made, a poem or the poetic use of language escapes the control of the author and takes on a life of its own, sometimes conveying meanings the author did not even envision.

Shakespeare's line allows room for multiple possibilities. For that reason, there is no one right way to interpret what it means, though there is clearly a wrong way: the literal one. By the exercise of his imagination, Shakespeare has released a series of meanings and potentially enriched the hearer's understanding of youthful judgments.[34]

On the other hand, when the word "green" is used in a scientific manner—say someone asks me to pass her the green pen—the word is intended to specify one and only one thing. The word "green" is employed to accomplish a task. In this case, it is important to control the "surplus of meaning" and ensure that meaning is univocal. Scientists even invent new words to avoid using any word or name to designate more than one reality.

At the heart of poetry is the metaphor: the "free invention of discourse"[35] by means of which two things, previously kept in different categories, are thrown together. The challenge to the mind is to seek in this absurd predication the point of likeness between them. The metaphor

32. Shakespeare, *Antony and Cleopatra*, Act 1, Scene 5.

33. I follow the new critics here who warn against the intentional fallacy.

34. As Ben Bradley wrote, "One of the joys of Shakespeare . . . is the infinitude of interpretations he supports." See "Shakespeare's Mighty Sorority."

35. Ricoeur, *Interpretation Theory: Discourse and the Surplus of Meaning*, 61.

generates a conflict of interpretations that is comparable to an enigma, and the act of interpreting the metaphor is comparable to the act of solving the enigma. The interpretation of metaphors demands of the reader a work in which the mind makes sense of absurdity by drawing out the relationship that links the realities in question, a relationship that can only be built on the ruins of a literal interpretation of terms. The encounter with a living metaphor—that is, a metaphor that is fresh and truly puzzling—challenges the ordinary way of viewing things. It offers the opportunity to discover a hidden kinship in the midst of conflicting and often puzzling interpretations.

The result of the living metaphor is the act of "seeing as." That is, in and through the linguistic invention that is the metaphor, one thing can now be seen as another. For instance, Seamus Heaney writes of the monks of old coming out of their oratory to find ordinary realities transfigured into objects used in worship: the waters before them, a smoking, moving censer; the grass, a fire.[36] By his metaphors, Heaney invites the reader or hearer of the poem to see these familiar objects of the natural world—the sea and the grass—as constantly offering praise to their Creator. With the monks, the reader, too, is enlightened and has an opportunity to join in the continuous acts of devotion offered by nature to its God.

Implications for Understanding Mary

The wager of this book is that proceeding via poetry and the surplus of meaning that it generates will yield fresh insights into the meaning and mystery of Mary, insights that cannot emerge by way of traditional Mariology. Traditional Mariology approaches the question of Mary through the works of the reasoning mind. There, the concentration is on "dogmas" or "doctrine": *Theotokos,* the perpetual virginity of Mary, the immaculate conception, and the assumption. These dogmas utilize what Paul Ricoeur calls "rational symbols," words or phrases that intentionally strip all that is figurative or embodied from an idea so that a purified concept can be employed in setting forth teaching. Dogma, then, is a distillation of meaning, accomplished through reason. From the rich, varied, and sometimes contradictory images and symbols by which the meaning was generated and in which it was heretofore preserved, the reasoning mind derives a truth and enshrines it as a teaching or a "doctrine" of the faith. Most often,

36. Heaney, "In Gallerus Oratory."

in the history of Christianity, such definitions of dogma have resulted from attempts to settle disputes over conflicting understandings of the faith. For that reason and others, dogmas or rational symbols are valuable and not to be discarded. If, however, they are not periodically refreshed by contact with the works of the imagination, they can stagnate and become stumbling blocks to a developing faith.

The affirmation of Mary as *Theotokos* (God-birther) is a good example. It served to explain and defend the belief that the two natures of Christ—divine and human—were united in one person, a position contested by Nestorius but ultimately victorious at the Council of Ephesus. In declaring her Mother of God and not just Mother of Christ (as Nestorius would have had it), the Council proclaimed that Mary gave birth to the one person, Jesus Christ, who is at once God and man. In this regard, Proclus of Constantinople praised her as "the workshop of the union of the two natures" and "living bush that was not burned by the fire of the Divine birth."[37]

When one resorts to images with such powerful ancestry as "living bush that was not burned," it is impossible to contain the meanings released. Soon enough, minds turned to what this says about Mary herself, not just what it says about the natures and person of her son. Speculation on Mary's very being soon followed and gave rise to questions about her own conception and holiness and even the reality of her death. In contrast to the earlier definitions regarding Mary, which were forged in the context of Christological controversies, the two modern dogmas—the immaculate conception and the assumption—developed not from conflict but from the burgeoning Marian devotion arising from attention to her life and mission.

In either case, however, once the dogma has been declared, the tendency in traditional Mariology is to use the "rational symbol," that serves as short-hand for the development, as the starting point, in the seeming belief that the narratives and images that funded the symbol can be left behind. Schooled by the work of Paul Ricoeur, especially in *The Symbolism of Evil*, I will show how a return to the narrative and images allows for both an expansion and a purification of meaning.

There is another difficulty attendant on the use of rational symbols in the proclamation and explanation of dogmas. While Christians believe that a central truth is affirmed and is to be accepted by faith at the time a dogma is proclaimed, we also acknowledge that the language used to proclaim the

---

37. Cited in Reynolds, *Gateway to Heaven*, 26.

dogma is time-bound, dependent on a given worldview and on the state of knowledge about the human realities ingredient to it.

For example, the term *Theotokos*—most often translated as "God-bearer"—literally means "God-birther" since *tokos* was a term used in medicine and "conjured up the experience of giving birth."[38] Now what it means to give birth will be presented differently by men who have not given birth and by women who have. It will be understood differently by people of the fourth century and people of the twenty-first century. Though the definition of Mary as *Theotokos* settled an important issue in Christology, it opens up vistas in thinking about the figure of Mary herself. Some would assert that it also led to an association of Mary with Isis, Diana, and other goddesses. While the title, *Theotokos*, might have been meant to tie things down and convey that Mary was the mother of Jesus, who was at once and inseparably human and divine, the use of the term set off depth charges in the devotional life of Christians; and, it still can.

My wager throughout is that by getting behind rational symbols or concepts to the symbols and myths that precede them, I can bring new light to the Marian dogmas. For this reason, the current study does not begin where traditional Mariology does. To continue doing so is to risk perpetuating misogynistic interpretations of Mary and of women that have become entwined in the interpretation of Marian dogmas.

Reconsidering the Imagination

To the popular mind, imagination is the capacity to "make things up." As such, it has been considered untrustworthy when compared to science or history, which are believed to put one in touch with "facts." Contemporary scholarship, however, reflects a growing awareness of the extent to which the imagination is active in the scientific method and in the work of historical interpretation. This thinking has led to a reevaluation of the imagination and its works, as well as to some important distinctions about the ways in which the imagination functions.

Products of the imagination appear in "texts." They can be linguistic (spoken or written), artistic (visual, plastic, dramatic, architectural, or musical), or ritual (sacraments or ceremonies). Some texts primarily preserve the work of the reproductive imagination; that is, the power of the imagination to produce images that copy or represent what is already known by

---

38. Cunneen, *In Search of Mary*, 130.

the senses. Others embody the work of the productive imagination, which generates a new way of seeing what is known by the senses and thus of revealing heretofore unrealized possibilities. It is this productive imagination with which I am concerned, for by it the faith advances.

The glory and the bane of the imagination is that all of us are influenced by the images we carry. By that I mean that unlike scientific objectivity that aims to separate and distinguish, the dreaming imagination calls on all that we have experienced and depends on all of it. For that reason, the interpretation of stories, myths, symbols, rituals, etc., will always betray the values—if not the biases—of the individual interpreter, the culture, or the period in history. The prejudices of men seem most likely to have been enshrined in the days before women joined the ranks of those offering interpretations and critiques of interpretation. Here is an example. Theodore of Mospuestia interprets the role of Mary at Cana thus:

> When the wine ran short, the mother of Jesus said to him, "They have no wine." His mother, as is the wont of mothers, pressed him to perform a miracle, wanting to show off the greatness of her son immediately and thinking that the lack of wine was a good opportunity for a miracle. But the Lord said to her, "Woman, what have you to do with me? My hour has not yet come." . . . In other words: "Why do you solicit me and make a nuisance of yourself? . . . I possess the power to work always, whenever and however I choose; even without being pressed by the needs of recipients I am able to display my power. Therefore, the excuse you allege of a lack of wine is an insult to me."[39]

This fourth-century thinker clearly thought all mothers were manipulative and interested in basking in the reflected glory of sons. A feminist lens will yield a very different interpretation of this biblical story, as we will see. At the same time, the feminist perspective can make the interpreter cautious about valuing positively some of the ideals that Christian tradition has historically valued, such as obedience, sacrifice, or—as in the Cana text—deference to another. Inasmuch as "all of us are influenced by the images we carry," the study of theology calls for a constant purification of interpretations so that prejudices or attitudes of exclusivity are not allowed to distort the saving truths of revelation. It also calls for the humility to acknowledge that when one deals with multivalent texts, it is not possible to claim that one has given the single correct interpretation. As Ricoeur has

---

39. Reynolds, *Gateway to Heaven*, 336–37.

taught me, interpretation is always a "wager."[40] Sometimes a given interpretation is accepted by the community and becomes part of the tradition of understanding, and sometimes it is rejected, either at the time or later.

The Feminist Critique

The movement for the advancement of women provided a powerful impetus for such purification of interpretations. The rising consciousness of women in the latter half of the twentieth century led to critical appraisals of the Marian tradition not possible before. Women who wanted to act and not just be acted on derided the image of Mary as passive, submissive, and docile. Women who sought an engaged and healthy sexual life saw the exaltation of virginity in the Marian tradition as impugning the holiness of women who chose otherwise. Above all, it seems, the enduring subordination of Mary—in the theological considerations of her roles—makes her a poor model for women who desire equality and long to exercise a capacity to lead.[41]

There is a significant difference between the Marian tradition and the Christological tradition, a difference of great import for thinking women. While Christ is understood by Christians to embody possibilities open to all (redemptive suffering, future resurrection, and even—in the Eastern tradition—deification), Mary has been treated as the exceptional woman whose privileges have little or no effect on the way other women are seen or understood. For this reason, a strong distrust of women in general, and an evident disgust with the workings of the female body, can coexist with—and perhaps be fed by—intense devotion to the Virgin Mother.

In addition, a naïve understanding of the way that symbols function has led to a simplistic application of complementarity to Mary and Jesus, as well as to the roles of women and men in the Church. The resultant "headship theology," whereby Jesus (and ordained men) represent the head while women (and laymen) represent the body, relegates all women in the Church to perpetual subordination. Favored by many in the hierarchy, this headship theology has raised serious objections from women theologians.

---

40. Ricoeur's concept of "wager" is discussed in Piguet, "Detranscendentalizing Subjectivity."

41. Johnson gives a sample of authors who make such judgments in her article, "The Marian Tradition," 120–21.

All of this means that a renewed theology of Mary must avoid the pitfalls of the past if it is to speak to women of the present. For the glories of Mary to be meaningful to believing women, they must reveal something about the nature of all women, not just the privileges accorded to one. If, for example, the Divine Motherhood is to inspire others to take up the responsibilities of parenthood, its holiness cannot be seen to consist in a miraculous virginity. For there to be true complementarity in the body of Christ, the roles and the mission of Mary must come to be seen as a dimension of the redemptive activity of God, in tandem with her son's.

It is no less true of feminists that all of us get into the interpretation of texts. We do not come to the Marian materials a blank slate. As I have indicated, Elizabeth Johnson approaches the topic of Mary with a determination to treat her as a historical woman and not a symbol, type, representative figure, or icon of anything.[42] Beverly Gaventa, who comes from a Protestant traditional point of view, discovers a Mary who is vulnerable, reflective, and counted among the witnesses of Jesus, but in no way finds the mystical Mary of traditional Catholicism. I openly confess that I am seeking evidence that the graced Christian imagination developed images of Mary that made her a match for Jesus the Christ; that is, images that reflected in female form one who is human to the utmost, to the point where humanity and divinity are united in her.

42. Johnson, *Truly Our Sister*, 100.

CHAPTER 3

A New Look at Ancient Texts

Introduction

As I HAVE ACKNOWLEDGED, the instances where Mary appears in the New Testament are very few; and of those, most occur in passages that have no corresponding equivalent elsewhere. The nature of these passages, however, is that they are rich in symbolism and echoes between the Old and New Testaments and between one Gospel text and another. For a people who heard the stories (as opposed to most of us who read them), these echoes would strike home and carry messages that may well be lost for us. In addition, many modern exegetes—who have been shaped in an ecumenical era and who are sensitive to Protestant accusations of Mariolatry—come to the texts about Mary with a set of assumptions: (1) Mary is subordinate to Jesus in being, role, and mission; (2) Jesus is all-knowing, even as a child, while Mary misunderstands and is in need of correction by her son; (3) there is a distinction between motherhood and discipleship, with the latter being the more important paradigm for Mary; and, (4) texts that pass the historical validity test are more dependable than one-of-a-kind texts, which are often considered to be of a fictional nature.

I propose to bracket the aforementioned assumptions and thus offer different interpretations of the texts concerning Mary. I am inspired to dare this by something heard at a lecture long ago: "We keep talking about the early Church. How do we know we are not still in the early Church?" In other words, developments that marked what we call the early Church might well mark our own time as well. As early Christians had to engage their tradition anew to understand what was being revealed, so might we as we consider the revelation about Mary in light of a new consciousness about being human, male, and female.

Just as revelation is carried by works, texts, and other objects made by human effort and creativity, so, too, does the apprehension of revelation require the ongoing and necessarily creative work of interpretation. As I have indicated earlier, all interpretation entails risk. It rests on what Paul Ricoeur called "a wager." My own wager is on the narrative quality of the texts about Mary. I will approach them with a certain hermeneutic of belief, not asking about their historical value but rather seeking to discern in them what is being revealed about the nature and role of this female character. Though there are important differences among the Gospel texts, in this instance I want to allow the imagination to move among them, making connections based on intuitions sparked by the language and structure of the biblical texts, by the experiences of women, and by the work of artists and poets who have their own ways of drawing out meaning from biblical scenes. The path has been paved for this by Sally Cunneen, who wrote in her own book on Mary:

> Old images, however, like old concepts, constantly need reinter-
> pretation. It may be especially hard for lifelong Catholics to see
> what Mary signifies, since our eyes are apt to be dulled by habit;
> taking the mystery of her role for granted, we may notice only
> surface details. Storytellers, poets, and painters who translate their
> deeper perceptions into verbal and visual forms can startle us into
> looking again.[1]

My guiding principle will be that of development; that is, the presupposition that as the communities of the New Testament struggled with events in their lives and matured in their faith, they also came to new realizations about the traditions that had been handed on. For that reason, I will begin the consideration of New Testament texts about Mary with the last Gospel to be composed and work backwards toward the earliest.

Musing on John's Gospel

Two stories in the Fourth Gospel feature the mother of Jesus and throw light on the nature of the adult relationship between Mary and Jesus: the

---

1. Cunneen, *In Search of Mary*, 310.

account of the wedding feast at Cana and that of Mary under the cross of Jesus with the beloved disciple. In the first, we find the mother of Jesus at a wedding feast, to which her son and the disciples have been invited as well. The supply of wine runs out, and the mother calls her son's attention to the fact by stating simply, "They have no wine."[2] In words that appear to be a rebuff, Jesus asks what possible concern that could be to either of them and pronounces that his "hour" has not yet come.[3] Nevertheless, his mother instructs the servants to do whatever Jesus tells them to do. In an about-face, Jesus orders the servants to fill with water the six stone jars in reserve for Jewish rites of purification. Following orders, the attendants fill them to the brim, which means there were six jars of twenty or thirty gallons of water. Next, Jesus commands them to draw some off and take it to the head steward. When they do as instructed the steward is amazed at the quality of the wine he tastes. Knowing nothing of its origin, he calls the bridegroom over to commend him for, as he says, "Everyone serves the good wine first and then the inferior wine after the guests have become drunk, but you have kept the good wine until now."[4] We are told that this, the first of Jesus' signs, reveals his glory. His mother is there to share in it.

If one carefully follows the text, one sees that Mary states a fact; Jesus asks a question. Mary takes the initiative; Jesus is reluctant. Though not the hostess at the wedding, Mary precipitates the saving action by her intervention. Though not the one who accomplishes the great sign, she is the one who notices the lack and moves to act for the good of those in attendance. Though the change in Jesus is unexplained, it is clearly there in his instructions to the stewards, which save the day and amaze those in the know.

The author of the Gospel, with all his artistry, has crafted a story of a man and a woman who cooperate to rescue a situation that could have thrown the whole festivity into chaos. Moreover, this scene occurs on the seventh day since the opening of John's Gospel, itself full of echoes of Genesis and the creation story.[5] For the poetic imagination, then, there emerges the new creation theme here in the narrative of the wedding feast with a

---

2. John 2:3.

3. John 2:4. I was told that one young (and tough) boy, when asked to tell the story of the wedding feast at Cana in his own words, told it thus: "Jesus and Mary and some friends went to this here party. Mary said, 'They ain't got no wine.' Then Jesus said, 'Well, hell. It ain't my party!'" In my view, this is not a bad translation, as well as being full of insight.

4. John 2:10.

5. See Thurian, *Mary: Mother of All Christians*, 120.

new Adam and a new Eve who, far from turning on each other, cooperate with each other to bring abundance and joy. There will be more on that theme later.

The musing mind might also make a connection with Luke's story of the finding of the child, Jesus, in the temple.[6] The story is that the boy Jesus, at the time twelve years of age, remains in Jerusalem when his parents set out for home and does not tell them he is doing so. The parents do not discover his absence until after they have gone a day's journey when they then begin to search for him among their relatives and acquaintances. When they do not find him there, they go back to Jerusalem.

After three days, they find him in the temple precincts, seated in the midst of the teachers, both listening to them and asking them questions. But then the text says that all who hear him are astounded at his understanding and his answers. Clearly, then, he is not just listening and asking; he is giving his own interpretations of the law and wowing the audience while he does so. When his parents see Jesus, they are amazed. It is the mother who speaks up immediately: "Child, why have you done this to us? Behold, your father and I have been so worried looking for you." "Why were you looking for me?" comes the reply. "Did you not know that I must be in my Father's house?" The text indicates that they did not understand the event about which Jesus spoke to them. The story ends with Jesus going back down with them to Nazareth to be obedient to them. His mother kept—with concern—all these events in her heart, and Jesus made progress in wisdom, maturity, and favor before God and men.

Most commentators see in this Lukan story a foreshadowing of the replacement of the earthly family with an eschatological family composed of disciples related to God. According to this reading, Jesus is upbraiding his parents for looking for him among relatives and friends when they should have known that he belonged to another father and would be about the business of that father's house. Read this way, 1) Jesus is in the know and his parents are in the dark; and 2) Jesus is right to have done what he did and his mother wrong to express her feeling. In other words, this reading makes Jesus the hero of the scene, a wonder-child teaching the doctors about the law and his parents about parenting.

This reading of the text puts the emphasis on the wrong place and misses something essential in the preparation of Jesus for his mission. We know from research into ancient texts that there were many stories of Jesus'

6. Luke 2:41–52.

childhood extant at the time the Gospels were compiled. Perhaps the most famous is the story of Jesus making birds out of clay and then breathing on them with the result that they flew away. It is quite possible that the story of the boy Jesus in the temple—the only story of his boyhood to make it into the canon—is intended as a corrective to those fantastic stories and to the human impulse to think that the child Jesus needed no formation from his parents.

Think of it this way: Mary and Joseph, having searched desperately for their young son, find him in the temple showing off for the doctors of the law. When the mother tells of the anxiety this has caused his parents, the child expresses no sorrow over what they have been through; but rather, he corrects her in front of the doctors of the law with a cryptic saying about being in his Father's house.

I once heard the poet Alan Shapiro describe how a still-maturing boy likes to imagine himself as already a man. What does Jesus' behavior say about the way he imagines being a man? He showed no care for the feelings of others, including his parents, even correcting them in front of others, and he acted on impulse regardless of the consequences to others or to himself (calling the temple "my Father's house" would be considered blasphemy in an adult). Given this interpretation of the event, one can understand that Mary is aghast at what she saw and heard. Note, however, that the text gives no indication of her responding in kind. As Sally Cunneen points out, Mary does not correct Jesus in front of others. We are told that the parents did not understand the event of which Jesus spoke; therefore, not understanding, they did not speak.

But they did act. Whatever the act of remaining in the temple reveals about what Jesus wanted at that stage of his life, the text says that he went back down with them to Nazareth and was obedient to them. The phrases have great meaning in Luke: He went back down to the low place where life is ordinary in contrast to the dramatic high place of the temple—to Nazareth, which might as well be Peoria, instead of to Jerusalem, not only the Rome but the Washington of its day.

In other words, Mary and Joseph said "No" to Jesus. No, you are not ready. No, you still have things to learn. No, that is not the way to serve God, not if it means that you have no feelings for others. It is up to us to imagine what transpired between this time and the public ministry and to figure out what they taught Jesus that made of him the man who related to simple people, poor people, the sick, outcasts, sinners, and women—especially to women—in ways that manifested such exquisite delicacy and depth of understanding.

If one connects the two stories—the wedding feast in John and the Lukan story of the boy Jesus, in both of which Mary plays a central role—these truths are revealed. As any child does, Jesus needed the guidance of his parents and they accepted this responsibility. After all, Mary and Joseph did not leave Jesus in the temple to be instructed by the scholars there; rather, they brought him home to be under their direction. Eventually, however, every parent also faces the moment when they have the opportunity to enter into a different relationship with an offspring. At the wedding feast, Mary signals that the time has come. She does not tell him what to do, but points to a need. This means that when Jesus begins his public ministry, he does not use his powers for self-aggrandizement; instead, he puts them at the service of others. Prepared for the moment by the upbringing of his parents, Jesus recognizes the "hour" and acts in concert with his mother, who has moved from the parental role to one of partnership.

The story of the wedding feast at Cana reads like an exquisite dance, with the partners knowing exactly what the other intends by what they say and do. It also constitutes something of a rite of passage as the mother hands off to the son responsibility for the welfare of others and the son not only measures up, but also astounds with the prodigality of his response to their needs. The flow will be reversed in the second and final story of the mother and son in John's Gospel.

In that Gospel scene, we find Jesus about to expire after the horrors of torture, the journey to Golgotha, and the crucifixion. In John's vignette, his mother and the disciple known as "the beloved" both stand near. Upon seeing his mother and the disciple, Jesus speaks to each. Using the form of address that echoes from Cana, Jesus says, "Woman, here is your son." And to the disciple, he proclaims, "Here is your mother."[7] The passage concludes by noting that from that hour, the disciple took Mary "to his own."[8] However, generations of interpreters—perhaps under the influence of their own experience—have translated that to mean the disciple took Mary "into his own home," which is exactly how the NRSV translates it. Yet "his own," as the Greek has it, brings reverberations of the opening of John's Gospel[9] where we are told that Jesus came into "his own" and "his own" received

7. John 19:26–27.
8. John 19:27.
9. John 1:11.

him not. Since Mary is given to the beloved disciple as "mother" and he to her as "son," however, it is equally possible for this to mean that the disciple took her to those who, like him, had become Jesus' "own."[10] Seen this way, Jesus is commissioning Mary to adopt a role with "his own", like the one she fulfilled for him: to mother the new community at the time when he was being taken from them. John's version brings to mind the stark passage in Mark where Jesus expands the meaning of family to include all who hear the word of God and keep it. Far from diminishing the family of the flesh, however, this Johannine text demonstrates that a mother's role can serve as a model for leadership in a community of faith.

Years ago, I read an account of a mother who went in search of the grave of her son, who had been killed in battle. After finally locating his grave, she made the journey to a military cemetery in the hope of at last standing over the place where her beloved son's body lay. When she arrived, however, she saw that all the graves were marked in the same fashion and appearing to be a seemingly endless row of markers planted in the earth. Suddenly, she had a change of heart. I can still remember her words (though I have failed to find the written account). "They look so alike this way," she said to herself. "I'll just think of them all as my sons." After many years and countless miles, she no longer needed to find the only one for whom she searched. This stretching of the mother's heart to include the fallen brothers of her son gives us some sense of what is being asked of Mary in her final appearance in John's Gospel. Perhaps she thought her work was over when she accompanied her son to the brink of death. Instead, in another and equally unexpected annunciation, she is asked to begin again in faith to give her life over to the designs of God.

Understood this way, John's text accounts for the final scene in Mary's life provided by the New Testament:[11] the scene that somewhat puzzled the authors of *Mary in the New Testament*. Mary is found in the upper room with the apostles, other women, and the brothers of Jesus. There, they devote themselves to prayer. On the day of Pentecost, when they are "together in one place," a mysterious event occurs.[12] Accompanied by a sound "like the rush of a violent wind . . . tongues, as of fire" appear and settle on each

10. See Jones, *The Women in the Gospel of John*, in which she cites Sloyan, "John," 211, where he also makes the connection between the use of "his own" in John 19:27 and John 1:11.

11. Acts 1:14.

12. Acts 2:1.

of them, filling them with the Holy Spirit.[13] Though Mary is not specifically mentioned as present on this day of Pentecost, traditional belief and the subsequent artistic tradition assure the faithful that Mary was still there, in the midst of Jesus' community, when divine power descended, just as it had come to her early in life at the time of the annunciation. Elizabeth Johnson objects that the artistic tradition all too often depicts Mary at Pentecost as the lone woman surrounded by the gathered apostles. The logical conclusion, she maintains, is that the "all" mentioned in Acts 2:1—"They were all together in one place"—refers back to the enumeration in Acts 1:13–14 where the presence of other women is clearly mentioned. Johnson blames this traditional representation on "an androcentric imagination."[14] A check on the images of Pentecost available on the internet, however, reveals a variety of versions: some with men only and some with two or three women accompanying Mary. Still, it is probably true that the most popular image, especially in the icon tradition, is that of Mary and the apostles. This need not be due to androcentrism, however. It is equally possible that the power of John's story of Jesus giving the community into Mary's care as "mother" resulted in the power and centrality of her figure in any imagining of the community (represented by the apostles) receiving the Holy Spirit. What remains for the people of God—then and now—is to work out the roles of each in the Church that is coming to birth and to ascertain whether or not they are gender-related.

Musing on Luke's Gospel

The Gospel of Luke concentrates on Mary's role in the conception, birth, and childhood of Jesus. After the dedication to Theophilus, the Gospel opens with a double annunciation. The first brings news of an impending birth to a barren woman, Elizabeth, who is wife of a priest named Zechariah. The word is brought not to Elizabeth, but to her husband, a pattern that is familiar from the story of Abraham and Sarah. The second annunciation is made directly to a young maiden, one who has "never known man" and one whom the text portrays as a virgin. From the first pregnancy comes forth John, who will be called the Baptist; from the second comes Jesus, who will be called the Messiah.

13. Acts 2:2–4.
14. See Johnson, *Truly Our Sister*, 299.

If, as some think, this gospel was written at a time when there were still those who claimed John the Baptist as Messiah, then the contrast between the pregnancies of Elizabeth and of Mary would be calculated to exalt Jesus over John and convince the hearer of his superior being.[15] Great as it is, the miracle of a barren womb made suddenly fruitful is trumped by the story of one who conceives despite never having had intercourse. Ensuing generations of male interpreters will pry the story of Mary's pregnancy loose from the context of this narrative and speculate wildly on the superiority of virginity over sexual experience and of Mary's womanly being over every other woman in history. To do so is to miss the implied comparison at work in Luke, a comparison that depends for its force on the realities and the symbolic potential of the woman's body.

The Old Testament tradition has many stories of women who were barren and then conceived: Sarah, Hannah, Rebekah, and Rachel are prominent examples.[16] In each case, God hears the prayers of the barren woman and sends a child, making up for the failure of the woman's body to function as it should. In the symbolic system of a woman's body, barrenness does mark failure. The clear expectation is that a woman should be able to conceive and that if she cannot, something has gone wrong.[17] In the case of Elizabeth—who was married, aged, and childless—the central symbolism is that of barrenness and hence, of a failure of human nature to function as it ought.

Virginity, on the other hand, carries no mark of failure. Virginity symbolizes many things: expectation, readiness, possibility, unexplored experience. But there is no failure attached to the symbolism of virginity nor cause for lament because the body is not functioning as it should. Moreover, in Luke's account, Mary gives no indication of having asked for a child; if anything, the invitation to conceive and bear takes her off guard. To God belongs the initiative; God comes to her. Dare one say that God needs her to accomplish something of importance to God's work in the world?[18]

15. See Brown, *The Birth of the Messiah,* 282–85.

16. See Gen 11:30; 1 Sam 1:5–6; Gen 25:21; and Gen 29:31.

17. It bears saying that there is no way to tell whether, in some of the instances cited, a problem on the part of the man accounted for the failure to conceive. Still, until very recently, all such failures were attributed to the woman.

18. Nicolas Cabasilas, the fourteenth-century Orthodox theologian, is one who so dared. He wrote: "The incarnation was not only the work of the Father, by His power and by His Spirit, but it was also the work of the will and faith of the Virgin. Without the consent of the Immaculate, without the agreement of her faith, the plan was as unrealizable

There is no question that in this scene Mary is experiencing a call comparable to those experienced by the prophets of old. She is, in the words of Paul Ricoeur, a "summoned subject," a "commissioned self."[19] Male-centered interpretations of this narrative have, for centuries, missed an amazing truth. This is one of the rare instances in Scripture where the challenge given to the summoned subject is something that only a woman can carry out: "You will conceive in your womb and bear a son."[20] Clearly, only a woman can fulfill this commission. That the woman who conceives is a virgin makes the narrative unique in the tradition of prophetic callings. At the same time, it connects this event to the promises of the prophets of Israel and Judah.

Mary's moment to confirm her fundamental option came when she was asked to mother the great one who would be called "Son of God." In declaring herself God's "slave," she gave her unreserved consent. Jesus faced a similar moment in the garden of agony when he realized what remaining faithful to his mission would demand of him. By crying out to the Father, "Not my will, but yours be done,"[21] he made a similar commitment to be God's slave, a characteristic that Paul would play on in the famous hymn of Philippians:[22]

> Let the same mind be in you that was in Christ Jesus,
> Who, though he was in the form of God,
> Did not regard equality with God as something to be exploited,
> But emptied himself,
> Taking the form of a slave, being born in human likeness.[23]

In another interplay, the overshadowing by the Holy Spirit promised by Gabriel in Luke 1:35 was not accompanied by a voice from heaven, though it did, nonetheless, mark Mary as a favored "daughter of God." Her experience is private; there is no witness. Her son's epiphany, on the other hand, takes place in an open space and in the presence of his cousin, John

---

as it would have been without the intervention of the three divine Persons themselves." Cited by Boss in *Empress and Handmaid*, 74.

19. See Ricoeur, "The Summoned Subject."

20. Luke 1:31.

21. Luke 22:42.

22. Johnson reviews contemporary objections to the use of this imagery in *Truly Our Sister*, 27. Still, both Mary and Jesus freely make themselves "slaves" to God and to God's desires, surely a different situation from other types of enslavement.

23. Phil 2:5–7.

the Baptist, who was perhaps surrounded by others. The author of the Gospel of John gives us the Baptist's testimony that he witnessed the descent of the Spirit upon Jesus.[24] Each will be guided by that Spirit, though that does not mean they will be spared the risk of human decision-making or the suffering of knowing their limitations.

Once the woman has consented to the mission, the conception, like creation itself, is "out of nothing," "de novo," and brings with it a new world. By this means, Luke's Gospel draws a line across salvation history, indicating where God has begun anew. Mary is not only enclosed within the new age, she initiates it with her act of faith, her "let it be done to me." With this, a new day dawns for humankind. It is a new creation. Essential to this new age is the willingness of a woman to give her body and the rest of her life over to the designs of God.

Having been assured that this conception, should she accede to it, will be accomplished by the mysterious power of God ("the power of the Most High will overshadow you"[25]) and also having been promised a sign by which she will know that this summons comes from God, Mary declares herself God's servant (literally, God's "slave"), willing to let be done what God's word will work in her. The biblical narrative makes it seem that the flow of this exchange was uninterrupted, and the decision made quite quickly. Artists and poets, however, understand that such a leap is not made easily and may involve hesitation or conflicting considerations.

24. John 1:32.
25. Luke 1:35b.

Meditating on Botticelli's "Cestello Annunciation,"[26] the poet Andrew Hudgins says that the artist gives Mary time. Time to reflect, to question the angel's words, to hear them inwardly, and then to reply as best she can.[27]

The biblical text and the gloss on it by painter and poet show a very thoughtful young woman whose freedom in the face of an awesome decision results in a moment of high drama. In her poem on this biblical moment, Luci Shaw reminds us that it could have turned out otherwise. Meditating on the experience of the annunciation, she sympathizes with the worrisome, delicate mission of the angel and the probable fear in the young girl.[28]

Luke the evangelist employs this drama to underscore the newness of what is coming. Everything depends on the consent of the maiden.

From this small biblical vignette, then, enormous theological questions arise. Was Mary free to say no? If she was, does that mean that God depended on her cooperation? If God depended on her cooperation, is Mary an agent in the redemption of the world? If Mary is an agent, does that mean that human beings are called to and capable of cooperating with God?

The poets cited above clearly think that Mary was indeed free to say "yes" or "no." Orthodox theologian John Jillions agrees and drives home the significance of such a position:

> Human beings created "in the image and likeness of God" are meant to be co-creators with God. Cooperation, collaboration (or synergy) between divine freedom and human freedom is part of the created order, and Mary's "yes" to God's call is the most powerful witness to this. God waits for her answer; he voluntarily surrenders omnipotence and becomes dependent on a human being.[29]

These interpretations enable one to hear that Mary's "yes" both prefigures and echoes an *obeisance* that her son will make in his time of dereliction: "Not my will but yours be done."[30] He will allow his body to be broken and himself to be put to death; she will allow her body to be filled with mysterious new life and herself to be committed to bearing and raising a

---

26. Botticelli, "Cestello Annunciation" (Tempera on panel, 1489–1490) in the Uffizi (Florence, Italy).

27. Hudgins, "The Cestello Annunciation," in *Upholding Mystery*, 106.

28. Shaw, "Annunciatory Angel," in *Accompanied by Angels*, 3–4.

29. Jillions, "Fr. Thomas Hopko."

30. Luke 22:42.

child who will be known as the Son of God. Both are servants of God. God has need of each in order to effect a new beginning.

Following the momentous encounter with God's messenger, Mary goes in haste to her cousin, Elizabeth. Unimaginable as it might be, Mary, the eminently sensible one, having been given a sign to confirm the trustworthiness of the angel's message, sets out to see if her cousin is, indeed, pregnant. Mary's arrival coincides with Elizabeth's quickening, which allows each woman to confirm in the other the power of God in their bodies: one impossibility corroborated by another. Elizabeth then greets Mary with words that will reverberate down the ages: "Blessed are you among women, and blessed is the fruit of your womb." Her next words associate Mary with the ark of the covenant, an association already made by Luke in the annunciation scene.[31] "And why has this happened to me that the mother of my Lord comes to me?"[32] As the truth of what is happening dawns on Mary more and more, she bursts into a song that draws on the words of a foremother who also called herself a handmaiden to God and who dedicated her son to a life in God's service: Hannah. The Magnificat, as the song has come to be known, gives insight into what is important to Mary as she receives these accolades.[33]

Mary is conscious of both her prior lowliness and her newly bestowed greatness due to what God has done in her. Here she stands in a long line of forebears called from obscurity to carry out some saving action that God has commissioned. She extols the mercy of God, rehearsing the ways God has "scattered the proud," "brought down the powerful," "lifted up the lowly," and "filled the hungry with good things" while sending "the rich away empty."[34] In all these ways, God kept promises made "to Abraham and to

31. The image of "overshadowing," used by Luke to explain how Mary conceives, harkens back to the mysterious cloud that "overshadowed" the ark of the covenant in Exod 40:34.

32. Luke 1:43. When David brings the ark to Jerusalem, he exclaims: "How can the ark of the LORD come into my care?" (2 Sam 6:9). In addition, Mary remains with Elizabeth for three months, as the ark stayed with Obed-edom for three months before it was brought to "the City of David" (2 Sam 6:11). I am indebted to Marina Warner for these connections, as well as the one above. See Warner, *Alone of All Her Sex*, 11–12.

33. *Magnificat* is Latin meaning "magnify." The title is taken from the first lines of the song: "My soul magnifies the Lord," as it is often translated. In an email exchange with me, author Carol Lee Flinders wrote that she thinks "to magnify" means to "enlarge the extent to which God's glory is *revealed* or visible."

34. Luke 1:51–53.

his descendants."[35] The Magnificat is the longest speech made by a female personage in the New Testament. It has been called a "war chant, God's battle song"[36] and "bellicose,"[37] but I prefer to avoid the language of war, thinking that violence does not necessarily accompany such liberating actions as those ascribed to God here. Seen retrospectively, from the vantage point of knowing the character and deeds of her son, it can be understood, as I have said, as a poetic prediction of what she will teach the child she carries: a child who will, as a man, eschew violence in favor of sacrificial suffering.

A most unusual depiction of the visitation scene by Jacopo Pontormo, located *in situ* at the atrium of SS. Annunziata, Florence, suggests a connection between the encounter of Mary with Elizabeth and the sacrifice of sons.[38] Above the painting of the two women, the artist has depicted the scene in which Abraham readies to sacrifice Isaac and to which several of the figures below call attention. In this way, Mary—who dominates the scene below—is associated with Abraham and the child in her womb with Isaac. In addition, the faith of Mary is subtly compared to that of the great

35. Luke 1:55.

36. Gebara and Bingemer, *Mary, Mother of God*, 22.

37. Warner, *Alone of All Her Sex*, 13.

38. See Hornik and Parsons, *Illumination Luke*, 58–60.

patriarch. Post-biblical theology will also relate God's sacrifice of the "only begotten Son" to the willingness of Abraham to do likewise. Here, then, Mary the mother is included in the line of the two fathers and her role in the sacrificial act of her son deftly implied.

Luke provided additional insight into Mary's lot at the time of the presentation of the child in the temple.[39] Simeon's words to her at this time drive home the reality that she will suffer because of her son and share her son's suffering:

> This child is destined for the falling and the rising of many in Israel, and to be a sign that will be opposed so that the inner thoughts of many will be revealed, and a sword will pierce your own soul too.[40]

One thinks of Matthew's story of the slaughter of the innocents in this regard.[41] How many mothers lost their infant sons due to Herod's determination to eliminate this Jesus? As Sister Wendy Beckett has observed, her son's being the cause of the deaths of many other children was surely one of the ways in which Mary's soul was pierced.[42] There would be others.

Simeon has seen the future and reveals it to Mary. In doing so, he prepares the way for her unique agony: an agony not in the garden but in the household. This talk of rising and falling is very close to the vision in Mary's own Magnificat. Now she has been told the cost of raising her child according to her lights and deepest convictions. The son will be contradicted by the powerful, the self-interested, the secure, the corrupt, the religiously smug, the hard of heart, the hypocritical; and a large part of her suffering will be to watch the effects of his upbringing on his life. From this time forward, she will carry the premonition of what lies ahead and make every determination in full consciousness of the fate to which she is sending her beloved child. Moreover, it will be her task to prepare him for the suffering to come in a way that will not rob him of his childhood. To give her son space to grow, Mary must forever relinquish her own girlhood.

---

39. Luke 2:22–38.

40. Luke 2:34–35.

41. Matt 2:16–18.

42. For a beautiful meditation on a depiction of the flight into Egypt from a Venetian Psalter of 1270–80, see Beckett, *Sister Wendy's Nativity*, 54: "Jesus, who is to end his life by dying for others, begins it by having others die for him. His safety is bought at the cost of a heap of mutilated babies, and his mother's happiness has been preserved by the terrible misery experienced by other mothers. Mary may have mourned for those other mothers all her life."

After the presentation in the temple, there will be no carefree moments for the mother.[43]

Musing on Matthew's Gospel

If we read Matthew's narrative in the light of Luke's, we see something similar at work. First, in the genealogy, Matthew includes five women, the last of whom is Mary. The four other women are Tamar, Rahab, Ruth, and Bathsheba. Their stories are important.

According to Genesis 38, Judah chose Tamar to be the wife to his son, Er. This son, however, was wicked in the sight of God; and as a consequence, God killed him. When Er's brother refused to give Tamar a child according to the dictates of the law, Tamar expected Judah to give her his third son, but Judah did not. Taking matters into her own hands, Tamar disguised herself and seduced Judah into having intercourse. She was careful, however, to keep a token of Judah's against the day when she would be discovered. When Tamar's pregnancy became known, Judah accused her of harlotry, but she was ready with the token that proved Judah the father. In this way, Tamar became the mother of sons.

The case of Rahab is more difficult. There is no comparable story of how she conceived Boaz, but we do know from Joshua 2 that she was a "harlot," so her union with Salmon was likely preceded by other sexual experiences.

In the book of Ruth, we learn that after Ruth's husband died, she was left a childless widow, a situation of great peril in her time.[44] Despite the pleadings of her mother-in-law, Ruth determined to remain with the mother of her deceased husband, an act of fidelity that brings her into the orbit of Boaz, a leader of the community. Having captured Boaz's attention and affection by taking the initiative to come to him in the night, Ruth conceives and bears a son.

---

43. I am aware that this interpretation puts the spotlight on Mary, despite the fact that Joseph was also present. Johnson has written eloquently about the significance of both parents being present in this scene (*Truly Our Sister*, 281–82). Simeon, however, addresses himself clearly to the mother, which I take to mean that she will be the one to carry the burden of knowledge and discernment.

44. Women in the Bible, "Who Were Ruth and Naomi in the Bible?"

Bathsheba, on the other hand, was wife to one of David's generals, Uriah.[45] Seeing Bathsheba bathing, David is consumed with desire, sends for her, and impregnates her.[46] In an attempt to cover up this sin, David calls Uriah home, hoping that he will sleep with his wife; but, the noble general will not avail himself of pleasures denied to his men and does not do so. David is then driven to send him to the front to be killed. In the wake of this treachery, David weds Bathsheba, but the child of their previous union dies. Bathsheba does bear another son, who is in the genealogy.

So, there are four women whose pregnancies are marked by deceit, prostitution, widowhood, treachery, and death; then along comes Mary. In the account of Matthew, Mary's betrothed suspects her of adultery, for she is pregnant before coming together with him. So far, it looks like Mary's story will fit in with those of the other women. However, the intervention of an angel convinces Joseph (and the reader) of her innocence. She has conceived "through the Holy Spirit."[47] Nothing negative marks the pregnancy of Mary. Her pregnancy, then, is not to be compared with the others but to be contrasted. Hers is of a new and different order.[48]

In each of the previous instances, the women in Matthew's genealogy had obstacles to overcome. The three who were married were clearly not barren, yet they had not been allowed to fulfill their duty under the law—one might say their mission as women—to provide a son for the people. Two were childless widows, and one was married to a man who was clearly more devoted to his soldiers than he was to her. Tamar and Ruth had been deprived of children by the death of husbands. Bathsheba was, for all purposes, raped by David and impregnated. David's punishment affected her, since the first child of their union died. Only after that loss was she allowed to raise a son. Rahab, as far as we know, was supporting herself by prostitution which, more than likely, meant she had no husband. Nothing is known of the circumstances of the conception of her son.

---

45. Bathsheba is not mentioned by name in Matthew's genealogy. There is only a reference to Solomon's mother who had been "the wife of Uriah," as told in 2 Sam 11.

46. Generations of male interpreters have written of Bathsheba as an "adulteress." There is no indication in the text that she initiated or consented to David's importunity. As a subject, she would not have been free to refuse the king. It is another instance where the woman is blamed for the man's sexual sin.

47. Matt 1:20.

48. It is also significant that the appearance of Mary in Matt 1:16 puts an end to the line of "fathers." "Mary of whom Jesus was born" is the surprising line.

The structure of Matthew's narrative creates a sharp contrast between Mary's experience and that of the four who precede her in the genealogy. She has not been robbed of children by death or deceit, nor is her conception marred by the "irregularities," to say the least, of her sisters.[49] She does not have to beg Joseph to give her protection. In Mary's story, the initiative belongs to God, protection comes from God, and the promised pregnancy, far from being marked by sin, will bring to birth one who will "save his people from their sins."[50]

The meaning I am drawing out is underscored by the citation of Isaiah in Matthew's narrative: "Look, the virgin shall conceive and bear a son, and they shall name him Emmanuel."[51] "Virgin," read in context and applied to Mary according to the signals given in the genealogy and the story of the angel's message to Joseph, means that she has no reproductive record. Mary brings no history of failure, death, deceit, hurt, disappointment, or any other negative to this moment. There is here no obstacle for divine power to overcome. The woman conceives as willed by God, and there is no stain upon it. Here, too, we meet the imagery of new creation, for the conception comes forth in direct response to God's intervention, God's messianic plan.

Note that the narratives do not draw a contrast between a woman who has not had sex and women who have. Even more important, there is no contrast here between the pure and the impure. "Virgin" in Luke is contrasted with "barren woman." "Virgin" in Matthew is contrasted with women whose pregnancies were achieved despite some other obstacles, which made the circumstances of their conceptions in some sense less than ideal. In the logic of these two New Testament texts, what makes this birth special, even "virginal," is not that it is not natural, but that it is in no way marred by human evil or a failure of nature.

The narratives of Matthew and Luke, then, adumbrate a vision of a new age, a new beginning. Perhaps it is not too much to suggest that the slate is wiped clean. In the new age, God will be revealed as never before, which will become clear as the respective Gospels unfold. The hero of the new age is clearly Jesus the Christ, but his coming is dependent upon one who has also been called by God for a mission of mercy. In a great reversal of the Genesis myth, the new Adam is brought forth from the new Eve, whose faithfulness and daring make possible the coming of a savior. Just as

49. This is a term used by Brown, *The Birth of the Messiah*, 74.
50. Matt 1:21.
51. Matt 1:23.

Eve came from the hand of God integral, alert to possibilities, and free from any history of failure, so is Mary imaged in the same way in the infancy narratives of Matthew and Luke. She is the virgin promised by Isaiah. Her greatness lies not in being free from some supposed taint of sexual experience, but in hearing the word of God and responding to it in faith and freedom. Artists through the ages have understood this aspect of the annunciation story and depicted the conception of Jesus as occurring through Mary's ear.[52]

The infancy narratives are not Greek myths. There is here no copulation with the gods, but rather a deeply Christian intuition of the Word of God embraced by one in whom it meets no impediment. As the God of Genesis created an entire world by the Word, so the God of Mary creates new life in her womb by overshadowing her. How it is done on the scientific level is not known. Such a question cannot be answered by the Gospel text for its purpose is not to provide biological information. What each Gospel offers is saving truth, and here the truth is that, through Mary, humankind has a second chance. In Mary, the faithful will see what cooperation with grace looks like in contrast to seduction by sin.

Musing on Mark's Gospel

What remains to be seen is the time of separation from a son under the influence of a radical movement. This is what Mark preserves for us—in all its starkness—in the two spare references he has to the family of Jesus.[53] Mark's Gospel alone retains the line that indicates his family thought Jesus had taken leave of his senses. They clearly come out of concern, in an attempt to rescue him from himself. Many assume that Mary was one of the family members who went to try to take Jesus away, though she is not mentioned in the text. It would be understandable, given his totally unconventional behavior. "This son . . . roams around through the country and creates unrest. He does things that are dangerous: danger threatens from the Jewish authorities and from the hated occupying power of the Romans. He puts *the whole family at risk*."[54]

52. As we will see, theologians before them had a similar intuition about Eve, maintaining that she "conceived the word of the serpent and gave birth to disobedience and death." See Reynolds, *Gateway to Heaven*, 55.

53. Mark 3:20–21 and 3:31–35.

54. Ben-Chorin, "A Jewish View of the Mother of Jesus," cited by Johnson, *Truly Our Sister*, 220.

Elizabeth Johnson notes of the passage in Mark 3:31–35, Jesus "emphatically 'rejects,' 'repudiates,' and 'disowns' his family using characteristic Jewish dialogue."[55] That interpretation is certainly consonant with the ordinary human experience of separation: the closer the ties, the more dramatic the break must be in order to accomplish something different from the expectations of society and of the family of origin. It is not unlike taking up a whip to cleanse the temple: a dramatic action that might make a point, but inevitably inflicts harm on those who are innocent. If this passage is read in light of the subsequent Gospel texts about Mary and Jesus, it is possible to speculate that Jesus learns to modulate this posture. Over the years of the public life, the fiery reformer morphs into the suffering servant, and the son—so ready to reject the ties of family—learns that the new and extended community must be based on the very values learned in the home at Nazareth. I imagine that the mother watched and prayed, trusting that the Spirit would lead him into the way that was right for the accomplishment of his mission. Others, however, see her as one who "misunderstood" and, as I have shown, read the later texts in light of that interpretation. They read this failure to understand back into the Lukan narrative of the finding in the temple.

Perhaps the experiences of learning to accept surprises and reversals—while watching one's child mature—can provide insight into Mary's struggles as mother and as servant of God. One such experience was related by a woman who attended Mount Saint Agnes Theological Center for Women. Her husband was an admiral in the United States Navy, and they had sent their son to the University of Notre Dame in South Bend, Indiana. As a member of a military family, her son had been raised to deeply respect the role of the military and to accept war as a regrettable necessity. One day, her son called home and said to her, "Mom, I heard a lecture by the most wonderful brothers. Their name is Berrigan."[56] This mother told the assembled group how painful the journey with their son was from that time on, as he became more and more convinced of the injustice of the Vietnam War. In time, the mother joined her son in this perspective, though her admiral husband was appalled and never reconciled to it. This story helped those of us studying Scripture together to imagine the ways in which Mary,

---

55. Johnson, *Truly Our Sister*, 217.

56. Philip and Daniel Berrigan were famous peace activists who protested the Vietnam War and, eventually, all wars.

who had been the teacher of her son, might have needed to learn from him as he matured and their roles changed.

It is equally possible, however, that Jesus is the one with something to learn. Perhaps he misunderstands at this point and needs time to incorporate his family into the new community he is seeking to establish. Testimony to such a development is found in the poignant Johannine scene under the cross.

The Emerging Picture of Mary

Reading the texts about Mary in a way that is supported by, but not limited to, historical research and that is enhanced by the intuition of artists and poets, as well as the experiences of women, results in a different idea of this woman. As a servant of God with her own call, issued directly to her by that God, Mary has a mission to fulfill. There is no competition between her motherhood and her fundamental election to "hear the word of God and keep it." Rather, her way of serving God and of discerning God's desires is in and through her motherhood and, though less is said of it, her roles as wife, family member, and neighbor. In this regard, she is entrusted with the awesome responsibility of raising a child who is divine but who must learn to be human and to exercise his powers in ways that will reveal what God is really like. In addition, the Gospel texts hold clues to a different reading of the relationship between Mary and Jesus. Despite contemporary efforts to depict Mary as a disciple and, at that, a disciple of her son, freed from Christological and societal assumptions, one can begin to see that, from the very beginning, the invitation to Mary comes from God and the response, whatever form it takes, will be to that same God. Mary has her own calling, as does her son. She has her own set of challenges and her own forms of suffering and triumph, as does he.

If we allow ourselves to be guided by the artists, we can discover a revealing interplay between the narratives concerning Mary and Jesus. It is an interplay that inspired artistic renderings. For instance, Judith Dupré writes of the Church of St. Savior in Chora, Istanbul:

> The church itself is dedicated to Christ and the Virgin. Within the church, the outer narthex corridor that portrays the scenes from Christ's life contains the inner narthex portraying Mary's life, and that in turn contains the central nave, also dedicated to Christ. This structural concentricity, also seen in the art program, reflects

the supernatural mutuality of Christ and his mother as the instruments of salvation.[57]

This lovely concept, "supernatural mutuality," is precisely what can be unearthed from contemplation of the sacred texts. If we move away from the isolation of one New Testament text from another—which has been imposed by the methods of historical criticism—and allow them to speak to each other and to us, "correspondences" reverberate and bring new insights into what the Church has preserved about Mary and her son. It will now be important to demonstrate that this supernatural mutuality obtains in the Church's prayer life.

57. Dupré, *Full of Grace*, 77.

CHAPTER 4

Marian Devotion Grows and Is Halted

Introduction

WE NOW KNOW THAT the Gospels developed backwards;[1] that is, the Christian memory and imagination moved from the vivid and detailed preaching of the death and resurrection of Jesus, through the time of his teaching and healing, to the beginning of his public ministry. Only two of the Gospels, as noted, trace Jesus back to the time of his childhood and birth, while the Gospel of John, which does not discuss infancy themes at all, traces him back to the beginning of the world. These narratives are rich in symbolism, draw heavily on the revelation in the Old Testament, and "supply a transition from the Old Testament to the gospel."[2]

The Protoevangelium of James

Something similar happens with the story of Mary's life, though it occurs outside the confines of the canonical Scriptures. It would seem as if the clues we have already studied provided a springboard for constructing a narrative of her life that paralleled that of Jesus. The Protoevangelium attributed to St. James, an apocryphal work of the second century AD, details Mary's conception, birth, presentation in the temple, and the delivery of Jesus.

1. Brown, *The Birth of the Messiah*, 26.
2. Brown, *The Birth of the Messiah*, 37.

Like holy women before her, Mary's mother, Anna, is childless. She laments her condition in a series of comparisons that show her desperation:

> Alas! Who begot me? And what womb produced me? Because I have become a curse in the presence of the sons of Israel, and I have been reproached, and they have driven me in derision out of the temple of the Lord. Alas! To what have I been likened? I am not like the fowls of the heaven, because even the fowls of the heaven are productive before You, O Lord. Alas! To what have I been likened? I am not like the beasts of the earth, because even the beasts of the earth are productive before You, O Lord. Alas! To what have I been likened? I am not like these waters, because even these waters are productive before You, O Lord. Alas! To what have I been likened? I am not like this earth, because even the earth brings forth its fruits in season, and blesses You, O Lord.[3]

God hears her lament and sends an angel to inform Anna that she will conceive and that her "seed shall be spoken of in all the world."[4] In gratitude, Anna promises that whatever child is born of her will be given to the Lord. In time, Anna brings forth a girl-child, whom she names Mary. From the time Mary is six months old, Anna protects her from all that is common or unclean. Meanwhile, Mary is blessed by priests and rejoiced over by parents.

Joachim is ready to fulfill Anna's vow when Mary is two years old, but Anna begs for another year to allow the child to break more easily from her mother and father. Accordingly, when Mary is three, she is presented to the temple where she will dwell until her twelfth year: the time of her maturation. At that point, an angel of the Lord instructs Zechariah, the priest, on the manner in which the spouse of Mary will be chosen. Each of the eligible men is instructed to appear with their rod. The angel's promise is that the Lord will give a sign. In due time, a dove flew out from Joseph's rod and over Joseph's head. Despite his reluctance—he, being of a great age—Joseph is persuaded to take Mary as his betrothed.

In the time between the espousal and the conception of Jesus, Mary is selected to work on weaving a veil for the temple. (The legend is that she is given the scarlet purple thread to work.)[5] Thus, the Protoevangelium ties

---

3. Protoevangelium of James, 3.

4. Protoevangelium of James, 4.

5. Williams has a lovely meditation on this dimension of the legend in "Weaving Scarlet and Purple," 57–74.

Mary's hands to the very veil that will be rent the moment when her son dies.

The story of Mary's encounter with the angel at the annunciation is clearly based on Luke's Gospel, but the meaning of his narrative is beginning to be fleshed out. Thus, the Protoevangelium says:

> And she took the pitcher, and went out to fill it with water. And, behold, a voice saying: "Hail, you who hast received grace; the Lord is with you; blessed are you among women!" (Luke 1:28). And she looked round, on the right hand and on the left, to see whence this voice came. And she went away, trembling, to her house, and put down the pitcher; and taking the purple, she sat down on her seat, and drew it out. And, behold, an angel of the Lord stood before her, saying: "Fear not, Mary; for you have found grace before the Lord of all, and you shall conceive, according to His word." And she hearing, reasoned with herself, saying: "Shall I conceive by the Lord, the living God? And shall I bring forth as every woman brings forth?" And the angel of the Lord said: "Not so, Mary; for the power of the Lord shall overshadow you: wherefore also that holy thing which shall be born of you shall be called the Son of the Most High. And you shall call His name Jesus, for He shall save His people from their sins." And Mary said: "Behold, the servant of the Lord before His face: let it be unto me according to your word."[6]

The Protoevangelium recounts Mary's visit to Elizabeth and her return to the home of Joseph, big with child. Thereupon the text melds the stories of Luke and Matthew, retelling the story of Joseph's dilemma and the subsequent dream that cleared things up for Joseph. New in this text, however, is the account of the priests who first accuse Joseph of having defiled the virgin whom they raised in the temple and then the account of Mary, having allowed herself to be defiled. Each, in turn, is given a lethal dose to drink as a trial before the Lord. Only when the dose fails to harm either do the priests accept the miraculous nature of the pregnancy and the innocence of the parties.

The growing belief in Mary's physical virginity, even after birth, is further emphasized in the tale of the midwives which is included in the narrative of Jesus' birth. The first midwife witnesses, with Joseph, the light-filled birth of the child of Mary. On her way home, she runs into a second midwife, named Salome, and tells her of the birth, by now described as virginal.

6. Protoevangelium of James, 11.

Doubting the story, Salome, in a scene reminiscent of the post-resurrection story of doubting Thomas, says she will not believe unless she has thrust in her fingers and searched the parts that would prove enduring virginity. She does so and withdraws a hand that is burning with fire, a punishment for her unbelief. When she begs for the restoration of her hand, by which she serves other women, she is instructed to take it to the child, who removes the punishment.

The remainder of the text is devoted to the visit of the Magi and the destructive rage of Herod, who has young males slaughtered in order to eradicate the threat posed by one of them. The Protoevangelium includes a narrative about Elizabeth, who succeeds in protecting the young John by praying that a mountain open up and enclose them, which it does.

Liturgical Development

We can see from this synopsis of the Protoevangelium that it is filled with incidents that are more magical than anything found in the canonical Gospels. How, then, can we know what, if anything, is important for Christian faith in this account of Mary's life. It seems to me that the best indication is what found its way into the Christian liturgy, for the public prayer of Christians is of great consequence for that "container of mysteries older than itself" that Catholics call tradition.[7]

The two events from the Protoevangelium that Christians have celebrated as Marian feasts through the ages are the birth of Mary and the presentation of Mary in the temple. (I consider it significant that, despite the tale of the midwives and subsequent attention to the question, there is no Feast of the Virginity of Mary. The celebration, when it occurs, will be of the immaculate conception.) The Feast of Mary's Nativity began to be observed in the first half of the seventh century and the Feast of the Presentation of Mary in the Temple by the end of the sixth century. Other Marian feasts derive from incidents in the canonical infancy narratives: The annunciation, the purification, and the visitation.

The Feast of the Annunciation most likely originated before or after the Council of Ephesus in 431 AD. Once the date of Christmas was settled on as December 25, the logical date for the annunciation was March 25. At one time in the history of the Church, the new liturgical year began on March 25, indicative of belief in that new beginning of which I have

7. Spretnak, *Missing Mary*, 88.

written. There was also a time when March 25 was always the date for Good Friday, a practice that suggested a dark side to Mary's acceptance of God's invitation and one that linked her passion to the passion of the Christ.[8]

The incident of the presentation of Jesus in the temple was also viewed as a Marian feast because of the belief that she was "purified" after the birth of Jesus at that time.[9] Though the earliest references (sixth century) to the feast describe it as celebrating the presentation of Jesus, the feast was renamed, in time, the Feast of the Purification of Mary. The Feast of the Visitation, commemorating the meeting of Mary and Elizabeth, appears sometime in the Middle Ages.

What we see developing out of the primary texts, then, is a set of feasts in which Mary's experience mirrors that of Jesus: The Nativity of Mary and the Presentation of Mary in the Temple. These feasts were accompanied by what many believe to be the oldest Marian celebration, based on the intuition that Mary was not subject to death in the ways of other human beings.[10] First known as the Feast of the Dormition, or the Falling Asleep of Mary, this feast eventually became known as the Assumption. Since the content of belief for this feast is that Mary was taken up to heaven, body and soul, one can see here a resonance between the assumption and the ascension. Two bodily presences inhabit the heavenly realm: one female and one male.[11]

These early Marian celebrations will eventually be joined by others that honor the female image of the mystery of the Christ: Our Lady of Sorrows, the Immaculate Heart of Mary, the Holy Name of Mary, and the Queenship of Mary.[12] In addition to these, there are feasts that honor Mary uniquely: the Solemnity of Mary, Mother of God; Our Lady of Lourdes, Our Lady of

---

8. Again, the artists intuit this truth. There are many depictions of the annunciation that include somewhere in the scene a suggestion of a cross or something symbolic of suffering.

9. In point of fact, the Lukan text says, "When the time came for their purification according to the law of Moses, they brought him to Jerusalem to present him to the Lord" (Luke 2:22). Note it says *their* purification," not "her purification."

10. Shoemaker thinks it can be dated to the later fourth century. See his "Marian Liturgies and Devotion," 134.

11. Jung considered the twentieth-century definition of the assumption as an article of faith to be the most important event since the Reformation because it elevated a woman, in all her bodiliness, to the presence of the divine. See his "Answer to Job," #752.

12. I am arguing here only on the basis of the feasts currently in the liturgical calendar for the universal Church. Marian feasts abound worldwide with devotions that are particular to countries and to religious congregations.

Mount Carmel, Our Lady of Guadalupe, Our Lady of the Rosary, and the Immaculate Conception.

Just as the Christian imagination eventually imaged Mary as the new Eve who is a match for the new Adam, this same imagination continued to supply images that make it possible to see Mary as a sinless child, a sacrificial offering, a holy mother, a faithful daughter of God, a suffering servant, and a triumphant queen of heaven. Here there is equivalence, not sameness. Yet, the praying imagination keeps finding new ways to relate Mary to Jesus the Christ.

Sarah Jane Boss points out a Vatican manuscript of the tenth century that includes a liturgy for Mary's birthday. One of the readings is Proverbs 8:22–31: "The LORD possessed me at the beginning of his ways."[13] The Gospel for the Mass is Christ's genealogy from the beginning of Matthew's Gospel, a genealogy that traces Jesus back to David. Boss calls attention to the way one modern commentator interprets the import of these readings:

> Etienne Catta describes this combination of readings as "striking," since it seems to suggest that the birth of the Virgin is analogous to Christmas, with Mary's creation from the beginning of time being rendered parallel to the Prologue to John's Gospel, whose opening words are: "In the beginning was the Word," referring to Christ. As Christ was present from eternity, and in the fullness of time became flesh in his mother's womb, so Mary was in some manner present from the foundation of the world, and likewise was born when the time was right for her part in the fulfillment of God's plan. Proverbs 8:22–31, in fact, came to be the standard reading at Mass for the feasts of Mary's Birthday (8 September) and of her Conception (8 December).[14]

Two things about this paragraph are remarkable. First, not even Pius Parsch, one of the foremost liturgical commentators writing before Vatican II, saw the significance of this combination of readings: one from Wisdom, indicating that Mary was in God's mind before creation, and the other, the genealogy of Jesus in Matthew's Gospel. About the latter, he writes: "The Gospel acquaints us with Joseph's illustrious lineage, which was Mary's too, at least in part."[15] Second, the change in the first reading for September 8, put in place after the Council, makes it even harder to understand how this

---

13. Prov 8:22–31.

14. Boss, *Mary: The Complete Resource*, 170.

15. Parsch, *The Church's Year of Grace*, 177.

is a celebration of Mary's birth. Now, the first reading is either Micah 5:1–4a or Romans 8:28–31. Neither of them connects with the Gospel reading in any logical way, nor is either of them about Mary or a female figure.

Despite the stripping away of Marian feasts that followed the Second Vatican Council, there are still, in the liturgical year, enough feasts remaining that we can espy the mirroring of Mary and Jesus. Let me list them:

The Birth of Mary (September 8)	Christmas (December 25)
The Presentation of Mary (November 20)	The Presentation of Jesus (February 2)
The Annunciation (March 25)	The Baptism of Jesus (Sunday after January 6)

or

The Immaculate Conception (December 8)	The Annunciation (March 25)
Our Lady of Sorrows (September 15)	Good Friday (Friday before Easter)
Assumption (August 15)	Ascension (forty days after Easter)
Queenship of Mary (August 22)	Christ the King (Sunday before Advent)

The Catholic Church celebrates the birth of only three persons: Jesus, Mary, and John the Baptist. In the case of all the other saints, the Church marks their day of death. The fact that the birth of Mary was long observed as a feast was one of the factors in the declaration of the immaculate conception, for it demonstrates a belief in her graced state at the time of birth. John the Baptist, while not believed to have been immaculately conceived, was considered graced at the moment he leapt in his mother's womb in the presence of the pregnant Mary.[16]

As I have noted, the feast on February 2 was originally a feast of the Lord; then became an observance of the "purification" of Mary after childbirth; and then, after Vatican II, was restored as a feast of the Lord. As such, it makes a nice parallel with the Feast of the Presentation of Mary. Each of them, Mary and Jesus, is imaged as having been dedicated to God at an early age, a dedication that shaped the rest of their lives.

The Annunciation, observed as a Marian feast as it was originally, makes a meaningful diptych with the Baptism of the Lord, for each feast celebrates the event at which the protagonist receives her/his mission and is overshadowed by the Holy Spirit. Though the Church has seen fit since Vatican II to declare the Annunciation a feast of the Lord, it can still be

---

16. Luke 1:41.

paired with the Feast of the Immaculate Conception, thereby making feasts that celebrate the first moment of human existence for each.

The remaining feasts need no explanation because the parallelism is quite obvious. Such clues in the liturgy of the Church point to the power of the Christian imagination to see one thing as another: in this case, to see Mary as Jesus and vice-versa. The difference in embodiment does not prevent the imagination from making connections, albeit connections that are metaphorical and thus require the mind to work at understanding. The contemporary tendency to dismiss this work of the imagination as of no value is to be lamented. René Girard has strong words in this regard:

> A great many modern theologians succumb to the terrorism of modern thought and condemn without a hearing something they are not capable of experiencing even as "poetry" anymore: the final trace in the world of a spiritual intuition that is fading fast.[17]

Private Devotion

The earliest known prayer to Mary is revealing in itself. It is the *Sub Tuum* and contains the words that are now echoed in a favorite Marian prayer, the *Memorare*: "We fly to thy protection." The usual translation of the Latin version of the original goes as follows: "We fly to thy patronage, O holy Mother of God, despise not our petitions in our necessities, but deliver us from all danger. O ever glorious and blessed Virgin."[18] In addition to the expressed belief in Mary's intercessory might and the use of the term, *Theotokos*, there is the remarkable fact that the Greek word *rysai* (deliver) appears in connection with Mary and is the same word used in the *Our Father*.[19] As Stephen J. Shoemaker notes, "Although the precise date of the papyrus [*Sub Tuum*] remains somewhat in question, most scholars are agreed that it was written in the latter part of the fourth century at the latest."[20] There are,

17. Beattie, *God's Mother*, 134–35, citing Girard.

18. See the entry, "*Sub Tuum*," in O'Carroll, *Theotokos*, 336.

19. O'Carroll, *Theotokos*, 336. It should be noted that, in time, the word "deliver" was eliminated, most likely because it suggested that Mary has the power to save. "Deliver" does not appear in the *Memorare*.

20. Shoemaker, "Marian Liturgies and Devotion," 130–31. This information sheds light on the presumption among some writers that devotion to Mary did not appear until after the Council of Ephesus in 431.

however, scholars who would date the prayer as early as the third century.[21] This prayer is important first, because it gives evidence of the inclination of Christians to pray to Mary as *Theotokos* and, second, because the appearance of the word "deliver" not only connects her to God in the Lord's Prayer, but also suggests a role for Mary in redemption.

Also of great interest is the account of the Collyridians.[22] This group, composed mostly of women, developed a ritual designed to honor Mary. Epiphanius (fourth century) writes of them, "Certain women adorn a chair or a square throne, spread a linen cloth over it, and on a certain day of the year place bread on it and offer it in the name of Mary, and all partake of this bread."[23] There is controversy among scholars about whether or not this is evidence that Mary was worshipped as a goddess. It should be noted that Epiphanius himself does not accuse the Collyridians of identifying Mary with God.[24] He is, however, opposed to the thought of women acting like priests.

Note that we have here a ritual that, like the Eucharist, consisted of offering bread; but this time, it is in the name of Mary. Does it give evidence of a respect, on the part of women, for the role she played in the story of salvation and/or of a desire to be related in prayer to one like us? No matter the case, the group was quickly declared heretical and the practice, whatever it was, fell out of use.

The Little Office of the Blessed Virgin Mary, which appeared by most accounts in the ninth or tenth century, gave Christians, monastic and lay, a set of prayers by which to honor Mary. Many of the prayers ask for her intercession. In those, Mary is praised as daughter, mother, and beloved. Of particular note are the antiphons that apply the Song of Solomon to Mary:

> While the King was at table, my spikenard yielded a sweet smell.
> His left hand is under my head, and His right hand shall embrace me.
> I am black, but beautiful, O ye daughters of Jerusalem; therefore, the King hath loved me, and brought me into His chamber.
> Now winter is past, the rain is over and gone: arise, my love, and come.
> Beautiful art thou, and sweet in thy delight, O holy Mother of God.[25]

21. O'Carroll, *Theotokos*, 336.

22. Beattie, *God's Mother*, 63–64.

23. Graef, *Mary: A History of Doctrine and Devotion*, 57, citing Epiphanius. Note that this date means that devotion to Mary predated the declaration at the Council of Ephesus, whereby she was declared *Theotokos*. See Beattie, "'Women full and overflowing with grace,'" 63.

24. See Shoemaker, "Marian Liturgies and Devotion," 132–33.

25. *The Little Office of the Blessed Virgin Mary*, 27, 35, 39, 43.

Other images from the Song of Solomon were applied to Mary in the course of centuries: "the rose of Sharon" (2:1), "the garden enclosed" (4:12), and "garden fountain" (4:15). It can only be imagined how much it meant to women to pray over these words, with their positive images of woman-hood, in a Church whose official liturgy was denuded of such references.

We have seen that the application of Wisdom references to Mary allows one to realize analogies between her and the Christ, so these selections from the Song of Solomon give rise to other musing thoughts about Mary. As scholarship on Genesis 2 has eliminated inequality from the relationship between Eve and Adam, so, too, has scholarship on the Song highlighted the mutuality between the male and female figures in this marvelous work. Seeing Mary as the beloved woman in the Song reinforces a notion of her as partner and not as a woman who is subordinate. The bride in the Song is articulate, takes the initiative, and is passionate about her love. Though the monastic tradition spiritualized the meaning of the language, the text of the Song still stands, providing for other generations images of an erotic relationship so free of domination that it can function as a metaphor for God's own love.

Phyllis Trible has shown that Genesis 2–3 provides a hermeneutical key with which to unlock the secret of the Song.[26] Ellen Davis, further-more, interprets the Song as the entrée to recovering what was once there for human beings: intimacy with God. She maintains that the exile from Eden represents the loss of intimacy in three primary spheres of relation-ships: between God and humanity, between woman and man, and between human and nonhuman creation. The Song, she writes, uses language to evoke a vision of healing in all three areas.[27]

From such trains of thought arise images of Mary as beloved of God, partner to her son, and mother of the cosmos. While much of the musing on Mary and the Song originated with monks and emphasized her virginity by capitalizing on the imagery of the enclosed garden, there is also in the Song, as I have said, an indication of what a redeemed eroticism would look like. A particular understanding of her virginity has kept the erotic off limits, where Mary is concerned. In a later chapter, I will suggest that it is time to rethink that. For now, I want only to note that the meaning of

26. Trible, "Love's Lyrics Redeemed," 144.

27. [O'Neill provided only Ellen Davis's name in the footnote. The probable reference is to Davis's article, "Reading the Song Iconographically."]

connecting Mary to the Song of Solomon can be enlarged and can, perhaps, remove some of the stumbling blocks to devotion to her.

Possibly the most ubiquitous Marian devotion among western Catholics is the rosary. The origin of this meditative prayer, named for a garden of roses (*rosarium*), is traditionally attributed to Saint Dominic, who is believed to have been given the prayer when experiencing an apparition of the Virgin. Most scholars only agree that the devotion appeared in the fourteenth or fifteenth centuries and, until the time of Pope John Paul II, varied little in form, structure, or content.[28] Based on the monastic practice of praying the one hundred fifty psalms, the rosary of old had three sets of fifty beads on which one recites the Hail Mary. The rosary that became most popular was a five-decade rosary on which three sets of mysteries could be said in sequence, rather than a rosary of fifteen decades. (A decade refers to a set of ten beads on which the Hail Mary is said, accompanied by a bead for the Our Father.) The whole chaplet is attached to a crucifix on which the Apostles Creed is recited, followed by a bead for an Our Father, three for Hail Marys, and another for an Our Father. This segment is usually attached by a medal of some sort with an image of Mary. During periods of persecution, there were even "ring rosaries" that could be worn on the finger and contained a single decade for praying.

While now considered a private devotion, there was a time, according to Nathan D. Mitchell's research, when the rosary was recited aloud in a fashion much like the Divine Office.[29] It was then that the Glory Be to the Father was added between decades and the Hail Holy Queen became the closing prayer. For this reason, the rosary was known as "Our Lady's Psalter."[30]

Praying with beads is a practice known to many religions, but what are known as "mysteries" distinguish the rosary from other forms of prayer with beads. These mysteries reveal, in an amazing way, the Christotypical understanding of Mary that I am pursuing in this study. For that reason, they deserve a closer look.

The Joyful Mysteries are comprised of the following incidents: the annunciation, the visitation, the birth of Christ, the presentation in the temple, and the finding of the child Jesus in the temple. Every one of the

28. See Mitchell, *The Mystery of the Rosary*, 1.

29. In 1971, Father Patrick Peyton, CSC, wrote to Pope Paul VI begging him to declare the rosary a liturgical prayer. See Thompson, "Vatican II and Beyond," 417.

30. Graef, *Mary: A History of Doctrine and Devotion*, 19–20.

Joyful Mysteries is solidly based on New Testament texts. In each of them, Mary plays a central role. The Sorrowful Mysteries are the following: the agony in the garden, the scourging at the pillar, the crowning with thorns, the carrying of the cross, and the crucifixion and death of Jesus. Again, each is rooted in a New Testament text; this time, Jesus is the central character in the scenes to be contemplated. The Glorious Mysteries offer for meditation the following: the resurrection of Jesus, the ascension of Jesus, the descent of the Holy Spirit, the assumption of Mary, and the crowning of Mary as Queen of Heaven and Earth. The first three Glorious Mysteries are based on scriptural texts; the final two are based on developments after the close of the New Testament and furnished by tradition; that is, by insights gained through imaginative reflection on scriptural texts. Contemplation of the Glorious Mysteries takes one beyond the pages of the New Testament. The structure is that Jesus the Christ is central in the first two; the Holy Spirit takes center stage in the third; and in the final two, Mary is featured. One might draw from this structure a foundational insight: Once the Holy Spirit has come, the Church is empowered to develop the tradition in ways that are faithful to Sacred Scripture and that bring the revelation of God in touch with succeeding generations and their ways of seeing the world.

Upon close examination, the symmetry of the rosary (as it stood before Pope John Paul II added the Luminous Mysteries) is quite extraordinary.[31] The Joyful Mysteries transport the one praying into the life of a young woman whose plans are disrupted by a call from God; who travels to the side of a cousin, a woman likewise surprised by joy; a woman who gives birth in difficult circumstances; who dedicates her child to God; and who experiences the terror and the triumph of losing and finding a child. The Sorrowful Mysteries call up before the mind's eye a man who undergoes an agony of decision-making, a flagellation, the humiliation of a mock crowning, the burden of carrying his own cross toward death, and an ignominious and tortured execution. In the Glorious Mysteries, each appears in triumph and the scenes are conjoined by the appearance of the Holy Spirit sent by one and received by the other: Jesus the Christ is raised from the dead and ascends to the right hand of God; Mary, his mother, is assumed body and soul out of this life and reigns with her son as Queen of Heaven and Earth. Herein, the mysteries of the Christian faith are contemplated

31. The Luminous Mysteries are as follows: the baptism of Jesus, the wedding at Cana, Jesus' proclamation of the kingdom of God, the transfiguration, and the institution of the Eucharist. For reasons that will become apparent, I am not including these mysteries in this study.

through the lives of a man (Jesus the Christ) and a woman (Jesus Christ's Mother, Mary).

It should be noted that the Song of Solomon plays its role in the shaping of the rosary. There, the bridegroom identifies himself as the "rose of Sharon" (2:1) and his beloved as "a lily among brambles" (2:2). The lily will eventually be replaced by the rose, echoing the groom's language.[32] The figure of Mary came to be steadily attached to the Song of Solomon because Mary was understood to be the primary bride of Christ. In this way, she became a model for each believer, as well as a type of the Church. By way of the metaphorical imagination, the Song could also be interpreted to mean that Mary is the enclosed garden in which the rose of the Christ is planted and grows. The incarnation itself could be cast in terms of this love poem: "The answer to man's Fall and Expulsion is God's entrance into the Mary-garden."[33] In the rosary, the story ends with the bride's reunion with the bridegroom in the heavenly realm. There they reign, as king and queen, in a restored paradise.

By the recitation of the fifteen mysteries, the devotee is subject to being drawn into a mystical realm where mother and son, male and female, bride and bridegroom, Scripture and tradition, past and present are not only joined, but also undergo an "admirable exchange" whereby one can be seen as the other. All of this is accessible to the laity because the rosary needs no priest or other mediator for its recitation. At the same time, the prayer grounds this mysticism in the doctrines of the Christian faith and, with only two exceptions, in the narratives of the New Testament.

No one knows exactly when and how the rosary took the form I have been studying.[34] It seems to me that it must have come from the depths of the community's contemplation and not be the product of the rationalizing mind.[35] That is why I lament the addition of the Luminous Mysteries. They bear the mark of the postmodern mindset and of a single consciousness, with the result that the beautiful symmetry that teaches so much about Mary and Jesus, women and men, and Scripture and tradition is disturbed, if not destroyed.

---

32. Winston-Allen, *Stories of the Rose*, 89.

33. Winston-Allen, *Stories of the Rose*, 92, citing Stanley Stewart.

34. Winston-Allen, *Stories of the Rose*, 65.

35. See Winston-Allen, *Stories of the Rose*, 74–75, for a chart of the many ways the mysteries were once configured.

Still the rosary retains its mystery and its power. Witness this passage from a writer who returned to the practice of saying the rosary after many years of neglecting it:

> It is, I now realize, the mystery of the rosary that has always com-
> pelled me, and not the form. At its core, the devotion is an enigma
> that somehow encompasses male and female, longing, radiance,
> and grief. It aligns a child's crystalline hope with Christ's shad-
> owy anguish, in a story which appears simple enough, bead after
> bead, but tugs at the spirit, as in an unexpected shift of light or the
> unanchored, airy sense one has when confronted with the radical
> unknown. The devotion pulls lightly at first, then more insistently.
> The telling of the beads begins mechanically; they are a puzzle.
> There is too much to keep in mind: the beads, the prayers, the odd
> stories with their baroque church histories, all prey to the jeers and
> emptiness of our culture.
>
> But after a while and with the telling, a certain silence comes.
> One tells the beads and scenes emerge, from the thirties, fifties,
> seventies, today. One sees these scenes and recognizes the rosary's
> great quiet, and its toughness.
>
> The rosary is not ethereal. It is not, in fact, for the fainthear-
> ed. "Pray for us now and at the hour of our death," we ask Mary,
> whom I once thought fragile, opaque, and hard to read. Now I
> understand her strength as she stands beside us, listening with us
> to the threshing cadences of the earth.[36]

A poem by John Shea further captures the role the rosary once played in the life of Catholics, with the added feature of reminding one that it often united men and women. Every night for thirty-seven years, Daniel and Mary O'Malley prayed the rosary together after supper. At each bead, he Hailed Mary, and his wife replied. When Mary died, he bore it well enough—con-tinuing their marriage chant, their evening embrace, within the repeated words of their prayer. But now he waited—for "Holy Mary, . . ."[37]

The Effect of Vatican II on Marian Devotion

There is clear evidence that the Christian imagination supplied the materi-als that enabled Mary to be seen as a female counterpart of Jesus the Christ and that the Christian faithful accepted these materials and incorporated

36. Conway, "The Rosary," 112.

37. This is the second of "Two Prayers of Loss," in Shea, *The Hour of the Unexpected*.

them into devotional life, public and private. It is not to be denied that there were also elements that could be interpreted as associating her with the Church, but those images coexisted with images that cast Mary as a woman called by God, given a mission, willing to suffer for that mission, transformed by that mission, and ultimately exalted by her God for unfailing faithfulness, all of which reflects, in the person of a woman, what we see in male form in Jesus the Christ. The imagination can function to embrace multivalences; it does not force one to choose between Mary as type of the Church and Mary as mirror of the Christ. Nor does the productive imagination simply put a woman in place of a man, as does the famous *Christa* in which a female form hangs on a cross. The mission and the manner of the woman differ; but at the same time, they offer a counterpoint to the mission and the manner of the man. (Though given what we learned from Ricoeur about Adam and Eve, this does not mean that the roles are inseparable and linked to sexual identity.) That mutuality of manner and mission is what makes the new Eve and new Adam paradigm so workable, in my estimation. This great stream of imaginative work was thoroughly diverted, however, at and after Vatican II.

The Council fathers were divided between what have been called, where Mary is concerned, the "maximalists" and the "minimalists." The former wanted a separate document to honor the Mother of God and were pushing for new titles for her. Their preference was for "Mother of the Church" and "Mediatrix of All Graces." The latter wanted Mary to be considered primarily as a type and member of the Church, even if a "preeminent" member.

By a very close vote, the Council fathers voted to include whatever was to be said about Mary in the document on the Church and not have a separate document on her, something the Protestant observers had let be known would be a disaster for ecumenism.[38] Chapter 8 of *Lumen Gentium* reads, at times, as if the Council fathers were looking over their shoulders for approval from the Protestant auditors, all of whom were men. Unlike the Catholic "auditrices," the Protestant auditors had free access to the coffee bars, where much informal consultation went on, and to the social gatherings where bonds were forged and opinions made known.[39] This access allowed them to have a great deal of direct influence at the Council.

---

38. Hughes, *The Monk's Tale*, 239.

39. See McEnroy, *Guests in Their Own House*.

In addition to an exquisite sensitivity to Protestants, there were other reasons adduced for including Mary in the dogmatic constitution on the Church. As stated by Cardinal Koenig of Vienna, they were as follows: The Church was the central theme of the Second Vatican Council; inclusion of Mary in *Lumen Gentium* would make it clear that Mary is not apart from the Church; it would also allow for an integration of ecclesiology and Mariology so that they complement each other; it would not overshadow or minimize the Christotypical dimension of Marian devotion; and the Marian titles, as contained in the litanies, arose from contemplation of the motherhood of the Church. Mary's saving role is like that of the Church.[40] These reasons do not highlight, though they might betray, other influences that led to the outcome regarding Mary: the biblical movement and the fear of Mariolatry on the part of some Council fathers from Latin America.

The "biblical movement" within the Church, ironically in some measure a gift of ecumenism, put emphasis on what is contained in Sacred Scripture and tended to cast doubt on anything that could not be found there. Moreover, the manner of reading Scripture was almost always that of the historical-critical approach, which downplayed—if not dismissed—whatever was considered "poetry."[41] It seems that some influential Catholic scholars determined to concern themselves only with "biblical Mary," with the result that "biblical-plus Mary," as Charlene Spretnak has termed it, was considered unworthy of credence and an impediment to ecumenism. At the same time, liturgists who might be expected to revel in the symbolism and poetry of the Marian tradition sought to purify the liturgy by a return to the patristic period. They read the new Eve/new Adam typology in the writings of the fathers of the Church as associating Mary with the Church and argued for a return to that paradigm. Even Godfrey Diekmann, who in his earlier book, *Come, Let Us Worship*, had called Mary the "echo" and the "image" of Christ, agreeing with the poet Charles Peguy that with the conception of Mary a "completely new chapter was begun in the history of mankind."[42] He even argued that "incorporation of Mary into the document on the Church would not downgrade devotion to Mary in the life of

---

40. Thompson, "Vatican II and Beyond," 411.

41. In the late 1960s when I began graduate studies, I had a noted Protestant professor of New Testament tell me that while I could read John's Gospel if I wanted, there was nothing of historical value in it. He dismissed the Fourth Gospel as "poetry" and never taught a course in it.

42. Diekmann, *Come, Let Us Worship*, 138, 140–41.

the Church, but put it in its proper context, ensuring a more solid basis of devotion rooted in biblical and patristic theology."[43]

In addition, there were problematic devotions to Mary that had become widespread in some parts of the world. Bishop Leo Dworschak reflected thus on the concerns of Latin American bishops:

> a goodly number of Latin American bishops have become frightened that a great many of their people have little religion left except a distorted form of a cult of the Blessed Mother which, in many cases, is material if not formal idolatry. They want to get the devotion to Our Lady into its proper perspective.[44]

Marian Silence

The years since Vatican II have been marked by an undeniable decline in Marian devotion among Catholics. Despite the fact that Paul VI used his authority to name Mary as "Mother of the Church," the image that has come to the fore in papal documents and in scholarly works of late is "Mary as first disciple," a title that underscores her subordination to her son. Neither of these titles, to my knowledge, has inspired works of art or hymnody.

Despite the optimistic prediction of Cardinal Koenig, the Christotypical dimension of Marian devotion has been severely diminished. As mentioned, feasts that were once Marian, such as the Annunciation, were renamed feasts of Jesus the Christ, and Marian feasts in the liturgical year were reduced in number and in significance.[45] The rosary, with its amazing symmetry between Mary and Jesus, was rendered unbalanced by the addition of the Luminous Mysteries. Images such as Cosmic Mary, whose mantle covers the globe, or Mary Refuge of Sinners, whose mantle welcomes those who are suffering from their own undoing, have been replaced by peasant Mary, even as Mary's motherhood has been underplayed in the emphasis on sisterhood.

43. Hughes, *The Monk's Tale*, 239.

44. Hughes, *The Monk's Tale*, 240.

45. Beaumont and Misrahi, *Days of the Lord*, 202, indicates that, prior to 1970, the Roman liturgical calendar contained nearly twenty Marian feasts. Since Vatican II, Marian feasts have been reduced in number; those that remain are relegated to one of three groups of greater to lesser "solemnity." The result is that there are now fifteen Marian feasts and eight of them have been assigned less importance than previously; in addition, of those eight, four are optional. See *Days of the Lord*, 368, note 20.

I fail to see how this change of images has been helpful to the advancement of women in the Church. To my mind, the subordination of Mary seals the subordination of women. It is time to reverse course and reconsider what was done at Vatican II by well-intentioned men who, though they wrote eloquently about tradition, subordinated tradition to the Bible, and whose eyes were fixed on the anticipated judgments of their separate brothers.

CHAPTER 5

The Blessed Assurance of Dogma[1]

Introduction

THE IMPULSE OF THE Christian community, when threatened by division or disagreement in its midst, is to gather the leaders for discussion leading to decisions. That is the ecclesial origin of Church councils, though political and social concerns also contributed to the calling of such councils. Up until the time of the Reformation, the dogmatic definitions involving Mary had arisen from controversies regarding the understanding of Jesus the Christ. Her titles of *Theotokos* (Mother of God), confirmed at the Third Ecumenical Council held at Ephesus in 431, and Ever Virgin (*aeiparthenos*), used to describe her at the Fifth Ecumenical Council held in Constantinople in 553, are related directly to affirmations about her son.

Of *Theotokos*, Orthodox Bishop Kallistos Ware specifies the connection, stressing that the designation

> has a precise and basic theological content. It is the safeguard and touchstone of the true faith in the Incarnation, emphasizing as it does that the child whom Mary bore was not a "mere" man, not a human person, but the divine person of the only-begotten Son of God, "one of the Holy Trinity," yet genuinely incarnate.[2]

Mary, then, is "she who contains the divine," and one can see how the title, Mother of God, given to her because of disputes involving her son, led to speculation about the woman chosen for such a mission.

1. This phrase originated with Lesslie Newbigin, *The Other Side of 1984*.
2. Ware, *The Orthodox Way*, 80, as cited in FitzGerald, "Mary the *Theotokos*," 84.

The infancy narratives of Luke and Matthew, with their imagery of a virgin who conceives, gave rise to titles for Mary such as "Blessed Virgin," "Holy Virgin," and "Ever-Virgin," which reflect a development from the scriptural narrative to the language of the creeds of Christianity where these encomiums appear. While applied to Mary, the titles have Christological import. Though the same Bishop Kallistos maintains that "Ever-Virgin" was used in a descriptive manner at the Fifth Ecumenical Council, with no doctrinal significance, the description (understood literally) implies that no other human being was involved in the conception of Jesus the Christ and that the same Jesus had no natural brothers and sisters—a belief that held until the time of the Reformation.[3] Thus, as Rosemary Ruether has observed, "Mariology has acted as an extension and safeguard of the doctrines of Christ's uniqueness."[4] The changes ushered in by the Protestant reformers, especially with regard to the privileged position of Mary, sowed the seeds of a rupture in any existing accord between Protestant reformers and Catholics on the understanding of the Christ stemming from earlier Councils. Over time this rupture has grown. In his St. Thomas More Lectures, Jaroslav Pelikan noted that:

> Protestant theology and biblical criticism have recast the theological doctrine of the person of Christ so basically that the agreement between the principal Reformers of the sixteenth century and their Roman Catholic opponents on the Christological consensus of the Councils of Ephesus and Chalcedon can no longer be taken for granted as a basis for discussion.[5]

The advent of the modern Marian dogmas also shifted ground once held in common. The definitions of the immaculate conception of Mary in 1854 and of the assumption of Mary in 1950 deepened the divisions between Protestants and Catholics, as well as between the latter and Orthodox Christians. Orthodox Christians do not deny the truth of these beliefs; rather, they consider a definition of dogma unnecessary. Among them, belief in Mary's sinlessness and in her dormition has ancient roots, celebrated in elaborate liturgies and preserved in traditional icons. For Protestants, on the other hand, the dogmas are contested on the grounds that they are not found in the Bible. The central issue, then, lies in differing stances on the question of development of dogma.

3. FitzGerald, "Mary the *Theotokos*," 85.
4. Ruether, *Mary: The Feminine Face of the Church*, 51.
5. Pelikan, *Development of Christian Doctrine*, 11–12.

Traditions of Belief in the Immaculate Conception

It is certainly true that, while the word "virgin" can be found in the New Testament as applied to Mary, terms like "immaculate conception" and "assumption" do not appear as such. Similarly, while Jesus is referred to as the "only begotten" in biblical language, the concept of "*homoousios*" or "of one substance" came later as a way of specifying meaning.[6] Recall earlier passages about the poetic and the scientific uses of language. Poetry allows multiple meanings to emerge, a situation that can lead to confusion if some of the purported meanings are contradictory or indefinite. Theologians concerned to protect the uniqueness and the sanctity of Jesus' birth began to ask, for example, whether the affirmation of Mary as virgin applied only before his birth or, indeed, also after his birth. Those who opted for the latter put forth the notion of perpetual virginity. This concept leaves no room for ambiguity, but it may also enshrine attitudes toward sexuality that will be considered outmoded or positively injurious by later generations. For this reason, Hans Küng could write:

> Doctrinal statements of the Church are, even though they have the assistance of the Holy Spirit, *human* formulations. As human and historical formulations, it is of the very nature of the definitions of the Church to be *open to correction* and to stand *in need of correction*. Progress in dogmas is not always necessarily just an organic development. Dogmas can even lead to a certain petrifaction of faith.[7]

Some of that petrifaction occurs when the leaders of the community forget that, as Rene Wellek has observed, "Christian doctrine is what the Church believes, teaches, and confesses as it prays and suffers, serves and obeys, celebrates and awaits the coming of the kingdom of God."[8] This means that the devotional life of Christians, as well as our reflections on experience borne of living out what we believe, have a place in the development of what the Church teaches.

6. Pelikan, *Development of Christian Doctrine*, 20, interprets John Henry Newman's logic regarding the connection between an understanding of Christ and an understanding of Mary thus: "Newman insisted that he who said *homoousios* with Nicaea had to go on to say *Theotokos* with Ephesus."

7. Küng, *The Council in Action*, 205, as cited in Pelikan, *Development of Christian Doctrine*, 145.

8. Wellek, *History of Modern Criticism*, 1–8, cited by Pelikan, *Development of Christian Doctrine*, 143.

John Kavanaugh, SJ, once drove this home in a sermon on the parable of the talents in Matthew 25:14–30.[9] The gift of God's revelation, he said, is comparable to the bequest of the talents. Those who have received this gift must not bury what has been revealed; that is, keep intact what they know by faith. Rather, revelation is given into the care of the Church so that believers might take the risk of enriching it with our own insights and experiences. In this way, revelation unfolds and stays alive. It becomes tradition, "the living faith of the dead," rather than traditionalism, "the dead faith of the living."[10]

Belief in Mary's sinlessness is instructive in this regard. Long before the declaration of the dogma of the immaculate conception, ordinary Christians found ways to testify to their conviction that the mother of Jesus was exceptional in holiness. Following a pattern of storytelling familiar from the Old Testament, apocryphal narratives of her conception appeared.[11] The essential elements remain constant. Mary's mother, Anna, was barren and longed for a child. Like Hannah and others before her, she implored God to have mercy on her and promised that any child conceived would be dedicated to God. Her husband, Joachim, offered sacrifice in the temple for the same intention. An angel appears to each, promising God's favor; nine months later a girl-child was born. These narratives reflect an incipient belief that God played a direct role in Mary's conception.

The feast celebrating Mary's birth also gives evidence of her exceptional holiness.[12] In the East, a Feast of Mary's Nativity can be traced back to the second half of the sixth century. A Feast of the Conception arose there in the seventh century. Michael O'Carroll writes, however, that the tradition goes all the way back to the fourth century.[13] It is clear, then, that Christian devotion to Mary led to a belief that she was not only free from personal sin, but had been preserved from any "stain" of original sin. It also shows that—as in the case of Christ himself—the Christian imagination

9. I heard John Kavanaugh give the sermon and remember it still.

10. Pelikan, *The Vindication of Tradition*, 55, also makes the point that "Tradition becomes an idol . . . when it makes the preservation and the repetition of the past an end in itself."

11. Reynolds, *Gateway to Heaven*, 331, cites the second-century "Protoevangelium of St. James, the Life of Mary," attributed to Maximus the Confessor (ca. 662), and the ninth-century *Libellus de Nativitate Sanctae Mariae*.

12. For all other saints (with the exception of John the Baptist), the day of death was kept as a feast.

13. O'Carroll, *Theotokos*, 180.

worked backwards to earlier and earlier stages of her existence. Eventually, her immaculate conception will connect with the idea of predestination, if not pre-existence.

The development of the doctrine of the immaculate conception, then, follows an interesting trajectory. The faith of the people in this privilege was evident; it was up to theologians, then, to account for the belief of the people in ways that corresponded with other central tenets of the faith. As Sarah Jane Boss writes, "the first thorough apologia for the belief that Mary's conception was immaculate (i.e., 'without stain') seems to have been written out of a desire to defend a liturgical celebration whose origin lay in devotion rather than Marian doctrine."[14]

The development of the dogma of the immaculate conception is thoroughly entangled with the developing concept of "original sin." Under the influence of Augustine of Hippo, many western theologians taught that all human beings come into the world affected by a sin inherited from Adam and passed on through conjugal intercourse.[15] Augustine was convinced that no conjugal act could be free of lust or "venereal pleasure," and it was in that deformation that he located the transmission of what came to be termed "original sin." Its locus was specifically in the seed of the male. While Catholic teaching on original sin is that it weakens but does not destroy freedom, this sin does make one subject to that defect of the will known as concupiscence. It is a defect that leads to actual or personal sins.

Given such an understanding of original sin, one can see why the virginal conception of Jesus became so important. Were he to have been conceived by a natural act of intercourse, Jesus himself would have contracted original sin and be in the weakened state of will shared by the rest of humanity. Such is unthinkable for one believed to be God-Man. It seems to have been equally unthinkable that his mother would have been a sinner. By this path, theologians could argue that Mary was never guilty of personal sin. The prospect of extending that freedom from personal sin to the moment of her conception and freedom from original sin, however, gave rise to disagreement among theologians. Thomas Aquinas and Duns Scotus are both representative. Though some of his writings indicated an inclination to accept the teaching about Mary's immaculate conception, Thomas

14. For a more complete account of this theological development, see Boss, *Mary: The Complete Resource*, 207–35.

15. See Pelikan's chapter on Cyprian in *Development of Christian Doctrine*, 73–94, for an explanation of why the tradition of the East differs somewhat on the question of original sin.

Aquinas was bothered by an important theological objection. If Mary was conceived without original sin, she would have no need of redemption by Christ; and Christ, in consequence, would not be the universal redeemer.[16] Duns Scotus obviated this difficulty by arguing that preservation from sin is superior to deliverance from sin.[17] Therefore, through his passion, Christ effected a more perfect form of redemption for his mother. While these debates raged, devotion to the immaculate conception nevertheless continued to spread, indicating that the piety of the people was little affected by the concerns of theologians or, in the words of Sarah Jane Boss, "that popular celebration was taking precedence over technical argument."[18]

By the nineteenth century, intensification of devotion to Mary, especially as the Immaculate One, coincided with papal privilege. In an era when the Church was determined to compensate for a loss of temporal power by a stronger exercise of spiritual power, Pope Pius IX anticipated the papal privilege of infallibility, later to be defined by the First Vatican Council. In 1854, after wide consultation with the bishops of the Catholic Church, he confirmed the belief that Mary was immaculately conceived. His papal declaration, *Ineffabilis Deus,* gives reasons for his action and traces the development of this conviction about Mary.[19]

The Pope calls upon the testimony of the liturgy, which enshrined the Feast of the Immaculate Conception in Christian practice. The Pontiff appeals to the ordinary teaching of the Roman Church and the ways in which his predecessors endorsed devotion to Mary under the title of the Immaculate. His text appeals to the tradition of the Church by demonstrating that the fathers of the Church rooted in revelation the belief about Mary's sinlessness by appeal to Genesis 3:15, where occur the words: "I will place enmity between you and the woman, between thy seed and her seed."[20] In this scriptural passage, they found evidence that Mary is joined to Christ in the battle against and in the victory over evil because she is "bound to Him by a most intimate and indissoluble bond."[21] Confirmation of her freedom

---

16. See Aquinas, *Summa Theologiae III*, q27, a2.

17. For a more complete study of Duns Scotus's argument for the possibility of conception without sin, see Boss, *Empress and Handmaid*, 128–32.

18. Boss, *The Doctrine of Mary's Immaculate Conception*, 212.

19. Pius IX, *Ineffabilis Deus.*

20. I use the translation that the declaration quoted as it appears in Palmer, *Mary in the Documents of the Church*, 82.

21. Palmer, *Mary in the Documents of the Church*, 83.

from sin is also found in the account of the annunciation, wherein Mary is called "full of grace" and addressed by Elizabeth as "blessed among women." In another reference to the fathers, Pope Pius IX observes that they compared Mary to Eve "while still a virgin, still innocent, still inviolate," and that they showed her superiority over Eve in a "variety of expressions and statements."

The Pope goes on to catalogue the ways these writers of the Church described her: the lily among thorns; the earth entirely untouched, virginal, undefiled, immaculate, ever blessed and free from all contagion of sin, earth from which was formed the new Adam; a flawless, bright, and fragrant paradise of innocence, immortality, and delights, planted by God, and fenced against every snare of the poisonous serpent; the never-fading wood that the worm of sin has never corrupted; the fountain ever clear and sealed by the power of the Holy Spirit; the divine temple; the treasury of immortality; or, the unique and only daughter of life and not of death, the offshoot of grace and not of wrath, which by the singular providence of God and at variance with established and ordinary laws, flourished and flowered, although sprung from a root that was corrupt and infected.[22]

The papal document then shows that—on the basis of the Genesis text, the analogy between Eve and Mary, and the flood of metaphors that filled their writings—these same fathers came to this conclusion:

> The same Blessed Virgin was through grace perfectly free from every stain of sin and from all contagion of body and soul and mind; that she was always at home with God and united with Him in an eternal covenant; that she was never in darkness, but always in light; that she was, as a result, a perfectly suitable dwelling place for Christ, not because of her bodily endowments, but because of her original grace.[23]

In the next move, the Pope gives an argument from suitability by showing it as "altogether proper" that the Mother of the Only-Begotten never lacks the "splendor of holiness."[24] In a final effort to provide support for the declaration, the Pope returns to the witness of the liturgy where "the Mother of God is invoked and proclaimed as the one spotless dove

22. Boss, *The Doctrine of Mary's Immaculate Conception*, 84.
23. Boss, *The Doctrine of Mary's Immaculate Conception*, 84–85.
24. Boss, *The Doctrine of Mary's Immaculate Conception*, 85.

of beauty, the rose ever blooming, perfectly pure, ever spotless and ever blessed."[25]

While I have not covered every dimension of the preamble to the declaration, the above references should suffice to show that the Pope, while exercising the privilege that allowed him to declare something true to the faith, was careful to provide a foundation for his action and for the truth he was proclaiming. In addition, these supporting arguments indicate that the dogma of the immaculate conception, while stated in terms of a concept equivalent to "original sin," derives from constant and profound meditation on the metaphors and symbols supplied by Scripture and the liturgy. The declaration itself is relatively brief:

> We declare, pronounce, and define that the doctrine which holds that the most Blessed Virgin Mary, in the first instance of her conception, by a singular grace and privilege granted by Almighty God, in view of the merits of Jesus Christ, the Savior of the human race, was preserved free from all stain of original sin, is a doctrine revealed by God and therefore to be believed firmly and constantly by all the faithful.[26]

One can see from the declaration how the language of poetry—e.g., "the lily among thorns," "a flawless, bright and fragrant paradise of innocence," one "never in darkness but always in light"—has received specifications as to time ("the first instance of her conception"), means ("by a singular grace and privilege granted by Almighty God, in view of the merits of Jesus Christ"), and meaning ("preserved free from all stain of original sin"). These specifications deserve attention.

Implications of the Immaculate Conception

First, while there have been times in Christian history when the soul was considered to be infused later than conception, there is no question that "the first instance of her conception" refers to the body of Mary. This teaching, then, holds that there is a true woman, conceived with a complete and genuine female body, who is exempt "from all stain of original sin." Despite the fact that theologians will subsequently insist that Mary is the great

25. Boss, *The Doctrine of Mary's Immaculate Conception*, 86.
26. Pius IX, *Ineffabilis Deus*.

exception,[27] logically it holds true that if there is one authentic woman who is undefiled by sin, then being a woman is not *essentially* defiled and defiling, as all too many have held in the past;[28] nor, I might add, can the natural functions of a woman's body be considered a source of "pollution." As a real woman, Mary would have experienced menstruation, childbirth, breastfeeding, and sexual pleasure.[29] If Mary is understood to have experienced these things and remained sinless, then we can finally separate the goodness of being created female from the distortions occasioned by misunderstanding and misogyny. Such an understanding requires a paradigm shift, but one that is of immense importance to a correct interpretation of what is revealed about the nature of women by the witness of Mary Immaculate.

April D. DeConick has observed that "misogynistic hermeneutics, theology, and social structures are the torrid byproducts of conceptions of the female body that made it a *naturally* deficient body."[30] The marvel is, then, that belief in the immaculate conception holds the promise that this sad history can be refuted and reversed.

The rational symbol of the immaculate conception needs now to be rooted once again in the flood of images that grace the proclamation. In addition, it must be separated from any notion that Mary is immaculate because she remains a physical virgin. The images of the proclamation and its supporting evidence hold before us the vision of a woman and of a womanhood that is at home with God, filled with light, undefiled, and shining with original grace. Belief in Mary Immaculate, then, counters any notion that woman's nature is an impediment to full participation in the divine life promised by Christ and realized in the process known as deification.

Second, the proclamation makes clear that Mary's freedom from original sin is an unrepeatable privilege accorded her because of the "merits of Jesus Christ." The idea that Mary deserved this privilege is put out of play. Original grace is just that: a gift to elicit rejoicing and thanksgiving. The song that Luke puts on the lips of young Mary at the time she visited Elizabeth attributes to Mary an awareness of this indebtedness: "He who is mighty has done great things for me" (Luke 1:49). The declaration, then, is

27. This is the meaning of the title of Warner's work: *Alone of All Her Sex.*

28. It is essential to believe that Mary is truly a woman, else the genuine humanity of Jesus be put in jeopardy.

29. There are surely ways Mary might have experienced sexual pleasure. The most likely is in nursing her baby, an experience that many women report to be intensely pleasurable.

30. DeConick, *Holy Misogyny,* 147.

in complete accord with the scriptural testimony to a woman who, in no instance, claims to have earned or merited in any way the grace that enables her to live as a flawless servant of God.

Third, any understanding of the meaning of the immaculate conception will be directly affected by one's understanding of original sin, for the essence of the definition is that Mary was "preserved free from all stain" of that reality. Clearly, the language here is metaphorical, for sin as a spiritual reality cannot leave a physical stain. Still, inasmuch as this imagery belongs to the realm of defilement,[31] the mind is led to conceive of original sin as something coming to a person from the outside, something passed on or contracted. Freedom from this "stain," then, will be imaged as purity, wholeness, or an undefiled state.

Because, in the long history of interpretation, the virgin was considered to be pure and undefiled, Mary's immaculate conception was readily linked to virginity. Perhaps it was, at times, unimaginable that a woman who has had sexual experience could be immaculate, given previous understandings of the link between sexuality and sin. Though there is a residue of the virginity imagery in the language of the proclamation of the dogma, it does not sound the dominant note. Rather, the images that fund the definition conjure up a woman whose being speaks of life, light, primal goodness, clarity, and abundant grace. In the mythical language of Genesis, Mary Immaculate shows us what it is like to be a woman untouched by "the fall," to exist as one who is totally at home with God, having no reason to hide or dissemble. While no other woman has received the grace of perpetual holiness, every woman has available to her the grace that restores and opens up a path to that holiness to which she individually has been called. For women seeking such holiness, Mary can truly be a "cause of our joy."[32]

Having moved back beyond the "fall," the imagination can then continue driving toward that formless void from which the very world was created.[33] It then becomes possible for Hildegard of Bingen to imagine Mary as the "earth" from which the new Adam is shaped, or the "waters" over which swept the creative power of God.[34]

---

31. See Ricoeur, *The Symbolism of Evil.*

32. From the Litany of Loreto.

33. For a beautiful reflection on this idea, see St. Anselm's sermon, "December 8: The Immaculate Conception of the Blessed Virgin Mary."

34. Cited by Boss, *Empress and Handmaid*, 84.

Mary Immaculate makes real, then, a new creation in which all of material reality participates in and through the incarnation of God accomplished in her very body. As is so often the case, artists lead the way in arriving at such insights. Sarah Jane Boss writes that there is an icon in an Orthodox monastery on the holy mountain of Athos which is known as "The Universe in the Womb of the Mother of God." It shows Mary's legs parted and veiled, so that the one looking on can see between them into the body of the Mother, where her womb holds the entire cosmos.[35] For this reason, Boss argues that "by virtue of the salvation which is wrought in the Incarnation, Mary is the instrument and partner by whom the original state of grace is returned to the creation."[36] This notion of Mary as partner to God is one that rises in Christian speculation only to be repeatedly ruled out of bounds because of a particular understanding of Mary's rise as threatening to the unique role of Jesus the Christ. One of the tasks of a renewed theology of Mary will be to reimagine this partnership in ways that accord with Christological definitions.

Tradition maintains that the conception at the heart of that incarnation is virginal. If, as I will show, one connects that virginity to her immaculate conception, the significance of what is termed the "virgin birth" lies precisely here: virginity is a metaphor for freedom from sin. It is that freedom that makes possible a birth that ushers in a new creation, giving human beings a fresh chance at life with God. A literal interpretation of the virgin birth reduces the power of the language and focuses attention on a miracle of nature rather than on the miracle of grace that is Mary's freedom from the deformations of sin.

The inescapable significance of this freedom for the mystery of the incarnation led Karl Rahner, one of the greatest Catholic theologians of the twentieth century, to write that Mary "stands within the circle of Christ's own predestination."[37] Here he is expressing something that the initial liturgy for the immaculate conception captured by selecting for the first reading Proverbs 8:22–31:

> The LORD created me at the beginning of his work, the first of his acts of long ago.
> Ages ago I was set up, at the first, before the beginning of the earth.
> When there were no depths I was brought forth, when there were no

35. Boss, "The Cosmos in Her Womb," 12.
36. Boss, "The Cosmos in Her Womb," 81.
37. Rahner, *Theological Investigations,* Vol. I, 210.

springs abounding with water.
Before the mountains had been shaped, before the hills, I was brought
  forth—when he had not yet made earth and fields, or the world's first
  bits of soil.
When he established the heavens, I was there, when he drew a circle
  on the face of the deep,
when he made firm the skies above, when he established the fountains
  of the deep,
when he assigned to the sea its limit, so that the waters might not
  transgress his command,
when he marked out the foundations of the earth, then I was beside
  him, like a master worker;
and I was daily his delight, rejoicing before him always,
rejoicing in his inhabited world, and delighting in the human race.

Prayer and devotion, then, connected Mary with holy Wisdom and, in
the words of Sarah Jane Boss, "give the impression of God's goodness being
present in creation from the beginning, and of his plan being fulfilled in
Christ through Mary."[38]

The liturgists of Vatican II, however, moved away from this association
of Mary with Wisdom. As is the case with other Marian feasts, the revisions
following Vatican II emphasized Christological themes. Thus, the reading
from Proverbs, which was formerly used for the Feast of the Immaculate
Conception, was replaced by Genesis 3:9–15, 20. Predestination to perpetual holiness is perhaps conveyed by Ephesians 1:3–6 and 11–12, also
read for the feast. The implication is that Mary is among all those chosen, in
Christ, "before the foundation of the world, to be holy and without blemish
before him." The singularity of her predestination, highlighted by Rahner,
has been muted by the liturgical changes.

Concluding Reflections on the Immaculate Conception

Before moving to a consideration of the dogma of the assumption, it seems
good to underscore a few points about the immaculate conception. First,
though some theologians wanted to confine Mary's freedom from sin to her
soul, the theological position that won out maintains that Mary's body is
included in this freedom. This position is clearly important for Christological reasons. Thus, as Sarah Jane Boss writes,

---

38. Boss, "The Doctrine of Mary's Immaculate Conception," 221.

Mary's conception is the beginning of the soul who will freely accept Christ into the world for the world's salvation. And her conception is equally the beginning of the flesh which is . . . united with the eternal Word of God in Christ.[39]

As is often true of doctrines, however, there are other implications here. The good news for women is that belief in the immaculate conception affirms that there is nothing inherently defiling about being embodied as a woman. The good news for all believers is that this dogma counterbalances an overemphasis on sin and redemption by giving strong expression to a dynamic of "delight and rejoicing in God's work of creation and redemption."[40]

A second point to consider is that there might well be a subterranean connection between the doctrine of the immaculate conception and the doctrine of the virginity of Mary. If this is made manifest, arguments against the immaculate conception, on the grounds that it has no scriptural foundation, can be refuted. Making this connection will entail recourse to a mode of interpretation other than historical criticism. However, in both cases—the immaculate conception and the virginity of Mary—thinkers find themselves confronted by doctrines that have been allowed to come unmoored from their originating images.

A third point to underline is the significance of prayer, especially liturgical prayer, in the development of this dogma. At work here is the mystery of Christian meditation, slowly ruminating on the powerful and complex metaphors and symbols of Sacred Scripture. From such meditation arose insights into the depths of revelation and a desire for feasts that honor Mary, including her role in salvation. Frequently, this process also led to an association of Mary with Wisdom, "the sole recognized female divine image in Israel."[41] While earlier ages seemed able to embrace this development, the modern Church—most likely with an eye to Protestant reactions—"purified" the Marian liturgies of all such associations. No longer do the faithful hear Wisdom readings on the feasts of the Mary's Immaculate Conception or of her Nativity. More's the pity, as the Irish say.

39. Boss, "The Doctrine of Mary's Immaculate Conception," 219.
40. Boss, "The Doctrine of Mary's Immaculate Conception," 233.
41. Schroer, *Wisdom Has Built Her House*, 52.

The Companion Dogma

As belief in the immaculate conception affirms Mary's holiness from the first instance of her existence, faith in the assumption of Mary avows the living presence of her whole being with the Godhead in eternal glory. This tradition of belief, too, has a long history, was made manifest in the praise and devotion of liturgical prayer, and culminated in a dogmatic definition that confirmed nearly universal belief in the assumption among Catholics. However, it did cause grave concern among Protestant observers and differs in that this tradition was informed by imaginative narratives that reconstructed the last days of the holy Virgin and pictured the destiny of her embodied being.

Stories of Mary's dormition, or "falling asleep," circulated as early as the fourth century.[42] According to most commentators, the narratives fall into two groups. In one, Mary's body is preserved intact in an earthly paradise but is awaiting reunion with her soul in heaven. In the other, Christ himself reunites her body and her soul. The texts show the tendency of the Christian imagination to draw parallels between Mary and Jesus. Thus, some accounts have her soul descending into Hades. Some recount that Thomas was not present at her death but returned three days later to find Mary's tomb empty.[43]

Walter J. Burghardt's masterful monograph on the testimony of the patristic age examines this "*Transitus Mariae*" literature, as well as early sermons and prayers, to demonstrate that the Christian imagination had no difficulty encompassing Mary's demise.[44] What seems to have been unimaginable was that her body, the body from which Jesus the Christ received his own, would be consigned to the grave and undergo corruption. By the sixth century, the churches of the East were celebrating a feast in honor of Mary's dormition. The prayers of these early liturgical texts express developing convictions about the mother of Jesus. A passage from the canon of Cosmas the Hymnodist is revealing:

> In conceiving God, O pure Lady, you carried off the prize of victory over nature. Still, in imitation of your Creator and Son, superior

---

42. For an account of this literature, see Shoemaker, "Marian Liturgies and Devotion," 134–37.

43. For a fuller account of these apocryphal narratives, see Reynolds, *Gateway to Heaven*, 295–96.

44. See Burghardt, "The Testimony of the Patristic Age."

to nature you bow low to the laws of nature; that is why, though you die with your Son, you rise to live eternally.[45]

Concomitant with this belief in Mary's risen life was the assurance of her intercession on behalf of those devoted to her. A prayer from the Roman or Gregorian Sacramentary testifies to this:

> Venerable in our eyes, O Lord, is this feast day, on which the holy Mother of God submitted to temporal death yet could not be weighed down by death's fetters—she who gave birth of her own self to your Son, our Lord, in flesh.
>
> Let come to the aid of your people, O Lord, the prayer of God's Mother; though we know that she has departed this life conformably to the condition of the flesh, may we experience her intercession for us in the glory of heaven.[46]

As the feast moved from East to West, "Dormition" was gradually replaced by "Assumption" and the issue of Mary's death receded, though it was not denied. Despite the skepticism typical of the Latin fathers with respect to apocryphal materials and their arguments against a too-ready acceptance of a bodily translation to the heavenly realm, by the seventh century, Pope St. Sergius I had added the Assumption to the other three Marian feasts of the Nativity, the Annunciation, and the Presentation or Purification. Later, Pope St. Leo IV ordered that the feast be preceded by a vigil and followed by an octave, or eight-day observance. This elevated the feast in solemnity and importance.[47]

Meanwhile, theologians considered the foundations for and the meaning of this growing devotion. As was the case with belief in the immaculate conception, there were those who were against it, for it, and uncommitted. Arguments against rarely involved an outright denial. Rather, theologians of this mind considered the assumption a pious hope rather than an article of belief. As for those in favor of the assumption, arguments varied. Mary's exemption from original sin liberated her as well from the punishment for sin; namely, bodily death and corruption. Her con-corporeality with

---

45. Burghardt, "The Testimony of the Patristic Age," 20. It is quite interesting to find the active tense of the verb, "rise," posited of Mary here. The tradition will eventually settle on the passive "was assumed," even as the former verb undergoes a change with respect to Jesus: from "being raised" to "rose." Either way, together Mary and Jesus incorporate both sides of the experience being sought in human language.

46. Burghardt, "The Testimony of the Patristic Age," 21.

47. See Pius XII, *Munificentissimus Deus*, 8–19.

Christ—that is, the fact that Christ received his human flesh from her and thus they shared life at the most profound bodily level—meant that Christ would not want her body to be subject to decay. Parallels were drawn with Mary's virginity: as God preserved her virginity in conceiving and giving birth, so would it be the divine will to preserve her body in death.

There is no record of anyone claiming that Mary's assumption could be proven from Sacred Scripture. Rather, biblical foundations for the belief were to be found in Old and New Testament types. The ark of the covenant, which was made of indestructible wood, and the bride in the Song of Solomon, who is called from Libanus to be crowned, were favorites. This passage from Isaac of Stella (1100–1169) gives the flavor of the prevailing typological interpretation:

> Today Mary went up from the desert of this world amidst the admiration of the Celestial powers who had never seen anyone go up from this world and take her place above all their choirs and their seats. Therefore, it is said: "Who is this that cometh up from the desert, flowing with delights?" (Canticles 8.5). These delights are the fruits of the virtues. . . . And since the blessed Virgin Mary, during her earthly life, exceeded all in the flowering of these virtues . . . so in that heavenly dwelling, comparable to the house of bread, she is filled with delights more than any of the others and with greater abundance, "leaning on her beloved" (Canticles 8.5), whom she felicitously formed, more in her heart than in her flesh, through her faith and her love.[48]

The major New Testament type was the woman in the book of Revelations, she who appears in the sky "clothed with the sun" (12.1), pregnant and crying out in birth pangs. This woman is considered a "type" of Mary of the assumption because of her cosmic setting and her victory over evil through the birth of a male child who is taken to God and to the throne of God.

One might wonder why, when this devotion was much older and the feast well established in churches East and West, the declaration of the dogma of the Assumption followed rather than preceded that of the Immaculate Conception. The main reason was that so many of the arguments for considering the assumption a revealed truth depended on Mary's freedom from sin at every moment of her existence. Once that belief was authenticated, it was possible for theologians to argue for the fittingness of

48. Reynolds, citing Sermo 52, in *Gateway to Heaven*, 320.

this privilege and to see her bodily assumption as the logical conclusion of Mary's earthly life.

After the declaration of the dogma of the immaculate conception in 1854, Marian fervor increased, as did the desire to see papal authority exercised on behalf of further honoring the Mother of God. By the time of Pope Pius XII (1939–58), the Vatican had received countless petitions asking that a dogma be declared regarding the assumption. It can sometimes be overlooked that Pius XII, in deference to the bishops of the world, consulted them before acting on those petitions. He asked each one to make known in a formal statement his answer to this question: "Do you, Venerable Brethren, in your outstanding wisdom and prudence, judge that the bodily Assumption of the Blessed Virgin can be proposed and defined as a dogma of faith? Do you, with your clergy and people, desire it?"[49] The affirmative response was, as the Pope himself writes, "almost unanimous."[50] This means that, while the declaration does reflect the exercise of papal authority, it also rests on the collegial consensus of the bishops, with the unquestioned support of the faithful.

The definition itself is found in the Apostolic Constitution, *Munificentissimus Deus*. From the opening lines, one can see the aftermath of World War II: "The most bountiful God, Who is Almighty . . . tempers, in the secret purpose of his own mind, the sorrows of peoples and of individual men by means of joys."[51] The Pope also refers, in the second paragraph, to "very severe calamities that have taken place." Theologians will take note of this context, and it will enter into interpretations of the belief itself.

Pius XII then acknowledges that the assumption is "closely bound" to the immaculate conception and that the proclamation of Pius IX regarding the latter increased the hope, on the part of the faithful, that the former would be defined as dogma. There follows a brief review of the sources of petition for this declaration and the information that bishops of the universal Church had been polled regarding it. It is the "outstanding agreement of the Catholic prelates and the faithful," writes the Pope, which shows

> the concordant teaching of the Church's ordinary doctrinal authority and the concordant faith of the Christian people which the same doctrinal authority sustains and directs [that] manifests this privilege as a truth revealed by God and contained in that divine

49. Pius XII, *Munificentissimus*, 11.

50. Pius XII, *Munificentissimus*, 12.

51. Pius XII, *Munificentissimus*, 1.

deposit which Christ has delivered to his Spouse to be guarded faithfully and to be taught infallibly.[52]

The text goes on to explain the guidance of the Holy Spirit, given to the successors of Peter. This assistance is bestowed, not so that new doctrine might be manifest, but so that popes "might guard as sacred and might faithfully propose the revelation delivered through the apostles, or the deposit of faith."[53]

Subsequent paragraphs adduce other evidence for this common belief: churches dedicated under the title of Mary's Assumption, liturgical offices in the form of feasts and prayers, and homilies in which Church doctors drew out the meaning of the belief, and the investigations of theologians over several centuries. All of this leads to the paragraph that sums up reasons for Pius XII to act at that moment:

> Since the Universal Church, within which dwells the Spirit of Truth who infallibly directs it towards an ever more perfect knowledge of the revealed truths, has expressed its own belief many times over the course of the centuries, and since the bishops of the entire world are almost unanimously petitioning that the truth of the bodily Assumption of the Blessed Virgin Mary into heaven should be defined as a dogma of divine and Catholic faith—this truth, which is based on the Sacred Writings, which is thoroughly rooted in the minds of the faithful, which has been approved in ecclesiastical worship from the most remote times, which is completely in harmony with the other revealed truths, and which has been expounded and explained magnificently in the work, the science, and the wisdom of the theologians—we believe that the moment appointed in the plan of divine providence for the solemn proclamation of this outstanding privilege of the Virgin Mary has already arrived.[54]

The Pope then expresses his own hopes for what declaring the dogma can achieve. He anticipates that it will increase devotion to the holy Virgin, patron of his pontificate; bring all who meditate on it to a greater realization of the value of human life; hold before the eyes of the world "to what a lofty goal our bodies and souls are destined"; strengthen belief in the

---

52. Pius XII, *Munificentissimus*, 12.
53. Pius XII, *Munificentissimus*, 12.
54. Pius XII, *Munificentissimus*, 41.

resurrection; and leave "a monument more enduring than bronze" of the Pope's own devotion to the Mother of God.[55] The actual definition is very brief:

> by the authority of our Lord Jesus Christ, of the Blessed Apostles Peter and Paul, and by our own authority, we pronounce, declare, and define it to be a divinely revealed dogma: that the Immaculate Mother of God, the ever Virgin Mary, having completed the course of her earthly life, was assumed body and soul into heavenly glory.[56]

It is masterful. The text does not define the question regarding whether or not Mary died a natural death; it does not interpret what the word "assumed" means; nor does it specify what is meant by heavenly glory. All of this is left open for subsequent speculation and development. What it does, however, is make clear that the *body* of Mary, as well as her soul, is in the heavenly realm and has been glorified.

Implications of the Dogma of the Assumption

Several aspects of *Munificentissimus Deus* deserve special attention. First, since debate over this definition has so often concerned the exercise of authority, it is important to note that the authority of the Pope is not exercised *over* the Church, but *within* the Church. The careful explanations of the beliefs and desires of the faithful and of the approval of the bishops give testimony to this. The Pope is not proclaiming a new teaching. What he is doing, in the words of Lesslie Newbigin, is giving "blessed assurance"[57] to the Church and to the world that the belief about Mary's assumption, which has matured within the Church, can be validly considered to have been revealed by God.

Second, the document proffers an excellent teaching regarding the role of liturgy in the development of dogma. Quoting *Mediator Dei*, Pius XII's own encyclical on the liturgy, the text shows that it is possible to draw enlightenment from this source because as "the profession, subject to the supreme teaching authority within the Church, of heavenly truths, [it] can supply proofs and testimonies of no small value for deciding a particular

---

55. Pius XII, *Munificentissimus*, 42–43.

56. Pius XII, *Munificentissimus*, 44.

57. See Kuhrt, "Proper Confidence in the Gospel."

point of Christian doctrine."[58] Moreover, the Pope explains, the liturgy "does not engender the Catholic faith, but rather springs from it."[59] For this reason, the rise of the Feast of the Assumption, with its prayers and homilies, gives important evidence of the faith of the people in Mary's glorification. This testimony becomes all the more important with respect to the assumption, because strictly speaking, scriptural evidence is non-existent, though there are indications in the liturgy that the conclusions regarding Mary's triumph over death are drawn from what Sacred Scripture has revealed. In this way, the assumption, like the immaculate conception, exemplifies what Metropolitan Kallistos Ware meant by stating, "The mystery of the Mother of God is *par excellence* a liturgical mystery."[60]

A third point, then, is that the definition of the assumption places in stark relief Catholic embrace of tradition as well as of Scripture. Tradition accompanies Sacred Scripture, aiding the Church's efforts to understand and to proclaim what has been revealed by God. The *Dogmatic Constitution on Divine Revelation* of the Second Vatican Council clearly states that "it is not from sacred Scripture alone that the Church draws her certainty about everything which has been revealed."[61] The dogma of the assumption, then, becomes a litmus test of acceptance of tradition as important to ascertaining the deeper revealed meanings of what is contained in the biblical texts. It seems to me that the hesitation to claim this dogma on the part of some contemporary theologians indicates a tendency away from tradition and toward Sacred Scripture as the only place to confirm genuine revelation.

A fourth point: as in the case of the dogma of the immaculate conception, the path to this definition was carved out primarily by lay piety, as Jaroslav Pelikan has observed.[62] While clerics might have given homilies on the feasts and been responsible for the theological reflections that ultimately conceptualized the belief, the devotion itself sprang from the love of countless women and men whose meditations, coupled with their own experience of family life, convinced them that the son's glory would be incomplete without the presence of the mother in glory with him. The history of the development of belief about Mary is replete with examples of insights

---

58. Pius XII, *Munificentissimus*, 16.

59. Pius XII, *Munificentissimus*, 20.

60. Cited in Levering, *Mary's Bodily Assumption*, 9.

61. Abbott, *The Documents of Vatican II*, 117, #9.

62. See Pelikan, *Mary through the Centuries*, 210.

from this kind of piety. It is an aspect of Marian teaching that a more cleri-cal, academic, and intellectual approach will come to disparage.

Fifth, it is possible to see, in the action of the Pope, an effort to counter the attitudes underlying the devastating treatment of the human body witnessed during the time of the Second World War. Accordingly, the definition proclaimed to all the destiny of bodily life: union with God. The body is not a carapace to be sloughed off before meeting the divine in glory. Mary's assumption holds out the promise of the resurrection of the body and of a life mysteriously but really embodied in the age to come. The Catholic novelist, Graham Greene, intuited this when he wrote:

> Catholics today cannot remain quite untouched by the general heresy of our time, the unimportance of the individual. Today, the human body is regarded as expendable material, something to be eliminated wholesale by the atom bomb, a kind of anonymous carrion.
>
> After the First World War, graves marked the places where the dead lay. . . . But no crosses today mark the common graves into which the dead of London and Berlin were shoveled, and Hi-roshima's memorial is the outline of a body photographed by the heat flash of asphalt.
>
> The definition of the Assumption proclaims again the doc-trine of our resurrection, the eternal destiny of each human body, and again it is the history of Mary which maintains the doctrine in its clarity. The resurrection of Christ can be regarded as the resur-rection of a God, but the resurrection of Mary foreshadows the resurrection of each of us.[63]

In this way, Mary's glorification represents the desired destiny of all of humanity. Her entry into glory opens the door for all those created in the image and likeness of God to come in.

It remained for the non-Catholic Carl Jung, however, to see a signifi-cance of the assumption unremarked, as far as I know, by Catholic com-mentators. Writing shortly after the definition of the dogma, Jung observed:

> I consider it to be the most important religious event since the Reformation. It is a *petra scandali* for the unpsychological mind: How can such an unfounded assertion as the bodily reception of the Virgin into heaven be put forward as worthy of belief? But the method which the Pope uses in order to demonstrate the truth of the dogma makes sense to the psychological mind, because it

63. See "The Living Spirit," *The Tablet*, 11 Aug. 2007, 17.

bases itself firstly on the necessary prefigurations, and secondly on a tradition of religious assertions reaching back for more than a thousand years. What outrages the Protestant standpoint in particular is the boundless approximation of the *Deipara* to the Godhead and, in consequence, the endangered supremacy of Christ, from which Protestantism will not budge. In sticking to this point, it has obviously failed to consider that its hymnology is full of references to the "heavenly bridegroom," who is now suddenly supposed not to have a bride with equal rights. Or has, perchance, the "bridegroom," in true psychologistic manner, been understood as a mere metaphor?[64]

There is no question that Jung saw in this definition an elevation, not just of a generic human being, but of a woman. That she is a bride "with equal rights" will be explored later.

Think of it. After centuries of defamation of the female body, the Church has declared that one of us—truly woman in all aspects—is with God in all her bodily glory.[65] Heretofore, this aspect of the dogma has seldom been brought out. In fact, the non-inclusive language that the Church persists in using, a language that requires substantial mind-bending, makes it all but impossible to concentrate on this aspect of the revelation. Take this passage from Pope Benedict XVI on the Feast of the Assumption in 2012:

> But we now ask ourselves: What does Mary's Assumption do for our journey, our life? The first answer is: In the Assumption, we see that in God there is space for man. . . . There is space for man in God, and God is near, and Mary, united to God, is very near, she has a heart that is great like the heart of God.[66]

A space for *man*? If that means human being, yes, but the most obvious reference of the dogma is that it enables us to see that in God there is space for *woman*. Belief in the assumption preserves the truth that nothing about the genuinely womanly body disqualifies for nearness to God, union with God. Moreover, it means that there are two human bodies in glory: the

---

64. International Marian Research Institute, *All about Mary*.

65. At various times, women were forbidden to receive Communion while menstruating, forbidden to touch sacred vessels, and forbidden to enter the sanctuary of churches, all from a conviction that the female body itself was a source of defilement and should be kept from places and things that were "holy."

66. Benedict XVI, "Assumption Day Address."

male body of Jesus and the female body of Mary.[67] This is the gem hidden in the definition of the assumption.

Conclusion

The two modern Marian dogmas did not result from disputes in the Catholic community; far from it. They arose from the desire of the people and their leaders to have the community's faith in Mary's immaculate conception and assumption proclaimed before the world as saving truths. At the time of each definition, the move to make belief in these privileges of Mary official was met with nearly universal approval and joy.

By the time of Vatican II, however, there surfaced among some theologians a reaction against the definition of the assumption. Joseph Ratzinger wrote:

> Since that day in 1950 a great deal has changed, and the dogma that caused such exultation then is rather a hindrance now. . . . We instinctively ask whether it is not really nonsensical, foolish, and a provocation to claim that a human being can be taken bodily into heaven.[68]

It is ironic that the assumptionist priest George Tavard came to this position, calling the "ethereal figure of a woman elevated to heaven" an "unfortunate and false illusion."[69]

One can only imagine what would have happened to the truths contained in Sacred Scripture if the canon had not been defined and preserved by the Christian community. At that, there have been efforts from time to time toward eliminating one or more books from that official list. The Reformers succeeded in doing so; and in any number of instances today, there is an unofficial "canon within a canon," by which certain texts are eliminated or ignored. Contemporary moves to treat the texts with suspicion have exacerbated the situation; yet the canon of Scripture stands, reminding any who would be so reminded that the Word of God is larger than the measure of our minds.

---

67. Note that the definition does not imply or state that Mary is the only human being in glory; it only assures the faithful that she, at least, is there and that being a woman did not prevent that glorification.

68. Cited by Levering, *Mary's Bodily Assumption*, 5.

69. Cited by Levering, *Mary's Bodily Assumption*, 5.

The dogmatic tradition of the Church functions in a similar fashion, guiding the community in its interpretation of revelation. In situations of dispute, as I have noted, the definition serves to rule out ways of understanding that would take the community off course and lead to erroneous conclusions. In the case of the Marian dogmas, where there was no debate to be settled, the definitions act to safeguard a core of truth so that it not be lost to future generations. Given the pressures of ecumenism and a misguided feminism, these beliefs about Mary, and implicitly about women, might well have been jettisoned. The challenge is to interpret them in a theological world that has idealized science and history, devaluing truths that are carried by works of the imagination; a world that until very recently has been shaped by the insights of male theologians, writing from their limited perspective; a world determined to make of Mary the exceptional woman—one with little in common with other women because of the extravagance of her privileges—rather than the exemplar of all that women can be.

CHAPTER 6

The Importance of Mary
as Shown in the Liturgy

"Liturgy is theology . . . the theology of the people."[1]

LAMBERT BEAUDUIN, OSB

As I LEARNED WHEN I began graduate school, it is usual for Catholics to know the Bible through the liturgy, rather than through reading the texts in their entirety and in full awareness of what distinguishes one from another. The liturgical year shapes the spiritual life of Catholics, even if the individual believer goes to Mass only on Sundays. The central cycle, of course, is the great story of the life of Christ: from anticipation of the Messiah in Advent; to his birth and childhood; to the baptism and public ministry; to his last days with its agony, arrest, crucifixion, and burial; to the resurrection and its aftermath: his transfiguration, ascension, and the descent of his Holy Spirit at Pentecost. This unfolding story is also punctuated by special observances of Christological devotions: The Holy Name, Divine Mercy, the Most Sacred Heart of Jesus, The Most Holy Body and Blood of Christ (Corpus Christi), Christ the King.

Within this central cycle, there are two companion cycles. Though liturgists conflate the cycle of the life of Mary with the celebration of the saints, calling both the "sanctoral cycle,"[2] I want to emphasize the importance of

1. Beauduin, *Give Us This Day*, 113.
2. Sanctoral Cycle, *New Catholic Encyclopedia*.

the Marian cycle, separating it from that of the saints. Beginning with her conception, the liturgy traces the important events of her life: her birth; the day when she was presented to the temple; the day she consented to be the Mother of God; and her visit to Elizabeth. Mary's life then coincides with that of Jesus the Christ on December 25, when she gives birth and his story begins. Her story terminates with the Feast of the Assumption that gives testimony to the Catholic belief that Mary, like her son, is—body and spirit—in the presence of God. Marian devotions also punctuate the story of Mary's life and celebrate her in ways that correspond to the titles and privileges accorded her son: The Most Holy Name of Mary, the Immaculate Heart of Mary, and the Feast of Mary Our Queen. In addition, January 1, once known as the Feast of the Circumcision, has been designated the Solemnity of Mary the Mother of God and is a holy day of obligation for Catholics.

Other feasts of Mary occur in the liturgical calendar for the United States: Our Lady of Mount Carmel, Our Lady of Sorrows, Our Lady of the Rosary, Our Lady of Guadalupe, Our Lady of Lourdes, and Our Lady of Fatima. Worldwide, however, the number of her feasts would be far more numerous, for many countries have a particular title for Mary, under which title they revere her.

In the Christological cycle, there is a preponderance of events record-ed in Sacred Scripture and a few celebrations that are rooted in Christian devotion and tradition. The situation is the reverse with Mary: only a few of the "events" of her life can be found in the Bible; most of them derive from Christian meditation on scriptural texts, as well as from traditions of prayer that sprang up in the wake of devotion to her. Is it possible that the liturgical pattern can give us insight into the biblical texts?

If we bracket, for a moment, the theological tradition that places one person in a superior position to the other, what can we see? I find an inter-locking narrative of a woman and a man: Both of them are conceived in a wondrous fashion, though each is born of woman, and each is dedicated in a dramatic way to God, as demonstrated by the matching presentation-in-the-temple feasts. The glory foreseen in the childhood of the man by an event such as the homage of the wise men—and the shadow cast over it, a massacre—and an episode where the child is lost invite speculation on how the woman, who was his mother, is affected by such events. The same is true once the mature man begins his public life.

Despite the silence that covers the woman while the Church is following the man's public life, she finds her place in a reading of Good Friday when the Gospel of John presents her beneath the cross of her son.[3] She has a central role in the great feast of Pentecost; and at the end, death does not claim her for she, like the man, is taken up from this life to the next in the totality of her being. The narrative line of each liturgical cycle concludes with the woman and the man being crowned, showing that each has achieved a fullness of existence.

With the single exception of Corpus Christi, the devotional feasts that concentrate on one or other aspect of the man's meaning for Christians are matched by corresponding feasts that show a similar significance for the woman. Thus, to the Feast of the Holy Name of Jesus, there corresponds the Feast of the Holy Name of Mary. Catholic Christians can have devotion to the Immaculate Heart of Mary, as well as to the Sacred Heart of Jesus. The relatively new Feast of Divine Mercy was preceded by the ancient Feast of Our Lady of Mercy.

What this examination yields is a series of observances that match the one to the other:

- Conception (December 8 and March 25);
- Birth (September 8 and December 25);
- Naming (September 12 and January 3);
- Presentation in the temple (November 21 and February 2);
- The sorrows of Mary and the passion of the Christ (September 15 and Holy Week);
- The Assumption of Mary and the Ascension of the Christ (August 15 and forty days after Easter);
- The Queenship of Mary and Christ the King (May 31 and the last Sunday of the liturgical year); and,
- The Immaculate Heart of Mary and the Sacred Heart of Jesus (August 22 and Friday after the octave of Corpus Christi).

This series of liturgies, with their attendant readings, hymns, and artwork, allow the faithful to see resemblances between them. Though

3. An earlier age made a connection between his sacrifice and hers by combining Good Friday and the Feast of the Annunciation on March 25, which usually falls deep in Lent.

differently embodied, and for that reason not subject to exactly the same experience, Mary and Jesus exemplify the apex of graced human existence. Being, as my mentor Felix Malmberg,[4] of happy memory, used to say, "Human to the utmost," they manifest humanity, male and female, totally united with the divine.[5]

4. Fransen, "In Memoriam: Felix Malmberg," 351.

5. It should be noted that the Marian feasts I have referenced are those that survived the purging of the liturgy after Vatican II when the Council fathers decided against any new titles for Mary, even against a separate document for her.

CHAPTER 7

The New Eve
Partner in Redemption

Introduction

WHILE DEVOTIONS TO MARY, liturgical and private, were evolving, accompanying theological developments took place. One of the most significant, for my purpose, was the paradigm of Mary as the new Eve. St. Paul was the first New Testament author to fashion the poetry of a brand-new beginning for the world by imaging Jesus as a second Adam.[1] His entire focus, however, was on the Christ; there is no mention of Mary as second Eve in Paul's writings. We have no way of knowing if Paul's contribution sparked a further innovation in the writers of the Gospels. What is clear, as I have shown, is that three of the evangelists constructed their narratives in ways that advance the theme of a new beginning, this time including Mary in that overture. Thus, the creation story is invoked; and with it, the suggestion of a man and a woman who will reverse the ancient curse and open new possibilities for humankind.

The Fathers of the Church

Several fathers of the Church, taken by the associations that could be made between Eve and Mary, developed what became an incipient Marian theology. Despite devoting great attention to the supposition that both Eve

1. The classical passages are Rom 5:12–21, and 1 Cor 15:21–22, and 15:45–49.

and Mary were virgins, the theology that arose did not concentrate on the physical integrity that defines virginity on the literal level. Instead, the early fathers linked virginity to obedience and spoke of each woman as "conceiving" a word: Eve, the word of Satan, and Mary, the Word of God. Thus, Saint Justin Martyr,[2] writing in the second century, could speculate as follows:

> Christ became man by the virgin so that the disobedience which originated from the serpent might be destroyed in the same way as it has begun. For while Eve was still a virgin and undefiled, she nevertheless conceived the word from the serpent and so brought forth disobedience and death. The Virgin Mary, on the other hand, received faith and joy when the angel Gabriel announced to her the good tidings.[3]

Virginity is the poetic symbol of being undefiled; but in this passage, it has nothing to do with a sexual temptation or with sexual intercourse. Justin is teaching, rather, that the first woman lost her innocence of being by rejecting God's word and taking into herself the word of the serpent. The new woman, the Virgin Mary, retains her undefiled status by enclosing within herself the Word of God. It is quite possible that, in order to suggest the new creation that undergirds the narratives of Luke and Matthew, each needed to tell the story of another virginal conception. In other words, if Mary is to be thought of as a new Eve, she, too, must be in a virginal state when approached by a "word" to be conceived.

Irenaeus continues this line of thought in the third century, developing the resonances between Eve and Mary and drawing far-reaching consequences from it. Irenaeus writes that Eve

> was made both for herself and the whole human race, the cause of death, while Mary . . . became the cause of salvation, both for herself and the whole human race. . . . Thus also was the knot of Eve's disobedience dissolved by Mary's obedience; for what the virgin Eve had tied up by unbelief, this the Virgin Mary loosened by faith. . . . [Therefore], the Virgin Mary became the advocate of the virgin Eve; and thus, as the human race fell into bondage to death through a virgin, so it is also rescued by a virgin.[4]

This remarkable theology, then, sees in Mary an exemplar of faith, not of non-use of sexuality. Moreover, she is clearly a savior, rescuing the

2. *Encylopaedia Britannica*, "Saint Justin Martyr, Christian Apologist."

3. Graef, *Mary: A History of Doctrine*, 17.

4. Graef, *Mary: A History of Doctrine*, 18, citing Irenaeus.

human race from bondage to death. Tina Beattie has argued persuasively that the loss of this important connection between Mary and Eve—a connection that makes of Mary "the advocate of the virgin Eve"—resulted in an injurious opposition of Mary the virgin and Eve the whore. By exalting Mary in her physical virginity and considering her the exception in womanhood, subsequent theologians drove a wedge between Mary and all other women, who were associated pejoratively with Eve.[5]

Instead, Beattie argues, the new Adam and new Eve theology holds the potential for "a doctrine of the incarnation in which sexual difference and the female body are accorded symbolic significance."[6] Beattie sees adumbrated a theological narrative in which Mary liberates all women from the oppressive consequences of the fall, "so that Eve and all the women of history are caught up and transformed in Mary's joy."[7] Needless to say, the Church fathers did not go there. Still, would that more theologians had followed Justin and Irenaeus in their deep understanding of the symbolism of virginity in the Scripture. Unfortunately, that was not to be the case. I will later consider the effects of this on Marian theology.

Some veered away from associating Eve and Mary. For instance, Zeno of Verona made a surprising move in which he switches from Christ/Adam and Mary/Eve to Church/Eve, concluding that Adam is redeemed by Christ, but Eve by the Church.[8] Eventually, this changed to Mary/Church, an association that would grow.

No one in the early Church left us a richer set of associations when it comes to Mary than the Syrian deacon Ephraim, who was called the "lyre of the Holy Spirit." He is the first to speak of Mary as the "Bride of her Son,"[9] a connection that we saw return in the application of the Song of Solomon to Mary. Mary is "a heaven for us, because she bears God"; like the burning bush, she "bears God in flame"; she gives "living bread instead of the bread of trouble, which Eve gave."[10]

Granted, many feminist theologians have decried this opposition between Eve and Mary. They maintain that contrasting Mary and Eve in this way results in seeing all women as one or the other. Thus, as the argument

5. See Beattie, *God's Mother, Eve's Advocate*, chapter 7.

6. Beattie, *God's Mother, Eve's Advocate*, 58.

7. Beattie, *God's Mother, Eve's Advocate*, 58.

8. Graef, *Mary: A History of Doctrine*, 44.

9. Graef, *Mary: A History of Doctrine*, 45.

10. Graef, *Mary: A History of Doctrine*, 45–49.

goes, a virgin-or-whore syndrome divides woman into two categories and considers individual women as all good or all bad.[11] That is certainly one risk of the new Eve theology. On the other hand, there are benefits to it that have not been brought to light since feminist biblical scholars have reinterpreted Genesis 2–3. A return to the scriptural texts that gave rise to this theology will yield fresh insights and unfold a different world for women.

The Revelation of Genesis 2–3

The imagery of Mary as the new Eve continued to nurture developments in Marian theology. It was associated with the belief in the immaculate conception, as well as with the conviction that Mary underwent her own form of resurrection and reigns in heaven with her son. From the Middle Ages right down to Pope Benedict XVI in the twenty-first century, theologians and popes continued to evoke the metaphor of Mary as the new Eve.[12] As long as the interpretation of Genesis 2 affirmed the superiority of Adam and the subordination of Eve, this metaphor did nothing to unsettle the relationship believed to have been obtained between Jesus and Mary, a relationship in which the woman is subordinate in all things. The work of feminist exegetes, too little adverted to in this regard, has done much to challenge this assumption of a hierarchical relationship between the original couple. In addition, a critical insight of the phenomenologist Paul Ricoeur provides grounds for contesting any simplistic application of the theory of complementarity to Adam and Eve or, by extension, to Jesus and Mary. As Alicia Ostriker has observed:

> If myths are basic human stories that encapsulate our deepest passions and yearning, myths also hold the key to the treasuries where our meanings for "male" and "female" are stored. When they are re-told by women, when the fabric is spun by women, everything changes.[13]

With the work of Phyllis Trible, everything changed for the interpretation of the second creation story in Genesis.[14] For centuries, commentators

11. Johnson gives a good summary of this critique in "The Marian Tradition," 122.

12. On the observance of the 2011 Feast of the Assumption, Benedict XVI said that, while our forefathers were defeated by the evil one, "Jesus, the new Adam, and Mary, the new Eve, finally defeated the enemy." See Benedict XVI, "Assumption Day Address."

13. Ostriker, "God the Mother," 140.

14. It is not the case that Trible's interpretation has gone unchallenged, but that

on Genesis 2–3 insisted that the story revealed the created superiority of men and the created inferiority of women, rooting in the Creator's will the domination of man over woman. Trible's work frees the text from that tradition, demonstrating that such interpretations stem from an androcentric bias. Her groundbreaking work of 1978, *God and the Rhetoric of Sexuality*, set a new course for the interpretation of the story of Adam and Eve.

Patriarchal interpretations assume that being created first, as was Adam, implies superiority. Coupled with the detail in the story that God took a rib from Adam and, with it, created a "helpmate" who is woman, this assumption led to the conclusion that woman is dependent on man for life: that her existence is derivative and not autonomous. Failure to distinguish the time before the incursion of sin from the time post-sin made possible an understanding of Adam's naming Eve that reinforces woman's subordinate status, as it was interpreted to indicate man's power over woman as willed by God. At the same time, in this school of thought, the powerless woman is blamed for leading the more powerful human being into temptation, which makes her responsible for the entrance of sin into the world, with all its consequent suffering.

From this classical interpretation issue a host of misogynistic statements that formed the attitudes of men for centuries and deformed the self-understanding of women. Tertullian's rant is paradigmatic:

> Do you not know that you are an Eve? The sentence of God on this sex of yours lives in this age. The guilt must of necessity live too. *You* are the devil's gateway. *You* are the unsealer of that forbidden tree. *You* are the first deserter of the divine Law. *You* are she who persuaded him whom the Devil was not valiant enough to attack. *You* destroyed so easily God's image man. On account of *your* desert, that is death, even the Son of God had to die.[15]

Against this long-standing tradition, Trible presses an argument for a different interpretation of the story. She advances by way of what she calls a literary study of Genesis 2–3.[16] Key to her explanation is the translation of the Hebrew word *ādām*. According to Trible, the word is not a proper name (Adam) but rather refers to a sexually undifferentiated creature that might be called "an earthling." Trible argues that sexuality does not enter

---

subsequent interpreters have had to take her work into account and concur with or counter it. See Yee, *Poor Banished Children of Eve*, 68.

15. Cited by DeConick, in *Holy Misogyny*, 123.

16. Trible, "A Love Story Gone Awry," in *God and the Rhetoric*, 74.

the picture until the moment when the woman is created. It is her existence that calls forth sexuality in the earthling, who can now be known as a man. Thus, sexually differentiated beings come into existence simultaneously; neither sex exists prior to the other. The transformation accounts for the cry of delight that escapes the lips of the man as he sees the woman: "This at last is bone of my bones and flesh of my flesh; this one shall be called Woman, for out of Man this one was taken."[17] It might be tempting to think that the phrase, "for out of Man this one was taken," implies inferiority. Trible insists, however, that the phrase refers to the raw material that God used, just as God used dust from the earth to form the earthling, 'ādām (a detail, incidentally, that does not make 'ādām subordinate to the earth). Of the woman, Trible writes,

> She is unique. Unlike all the rest of creation, she does not come from the earth; rather, Yahweh God *builds* the rib into woman. The Hebrew verb *build* (*banah*) indicates considerable labor to produce solid results. Hence, woman is no weak, dainty, ephemeral creature. No opposite sex, no second sex, no derived sex; in short, no "Adam's rib." Instead, woman is the culmination of creation, fulfilling humanity in sexuality. Equal in creation with the man, she is, at this point, elevated in emphasis by the design of the story.[18]

This beautiful portrait will be destroyed by sin. Trible's study of the text clearly reveals that there is manifold responsibility for that destruction: the man, the woman, and the serpent are punished and, therefore, held accountable. Each punishment is unique to the subject. Each subject is considered a moral agent.

Trible interprets the punishment of Eve as leading to the state of domination that earlier exegetes had read into the original creation. She writes that even after the man has betrayed the woman to God,

> she still yearns for the original unity of male and female. The man will not reciprocate the woman's desire; instead, he will rule over her. Thus, she lives in unresolved tension. Where once there was mutuality, now there is a hierarchy of division. The man dominates the woman to pervert sexuality. Hence, the woman is corrupted in becoming a slave, and the man is corrupted in becoming a master. His supremacy is neither a divine right nor a male prerogative. Her

17. Gen 2:23.
18. Trible, *God and the Rhetoric*, 102.

subordination is neither a divine decree nor the female destiny. Both their positions result from shared disobedience.[19]

What emerges from the work of Phyllis Trible is an image of the original creation in which the male and the female exist in a state of difference without preference. That is, one way of being is not superior to the other; each can take delight in the difference; and each is drawn to the other by that difference. It is this primal state that is disrupted by the chain of events which then leads to their hiding in shame from the creator God and to their turning on one another.

The phenomenologist Paul Ricoeur reached similar conclusions by a different method in his magisterial work *The Symbolism of Evil.* As he was working out a philosophy of the will, of which *The Symbolism of Evil* constituted a second volume, Ricoeur's interests in the myth were somewhat different from those of Trible. He was particularly fascinated by the transition from the time of innocence to the time of guilt, and he brought his analysis to bear on that point. Since, according to the myth, Eve is the "weak point," the point of entrée for evil, she represents something that is not peculiar to women but to all of humanity: the frailty of the human. Ricoeur maintains that evil is possible through human freedom and that, in the myth, the woman represents "the point of least resistance of finite freedom to the appeal of the *Pseudo,* of the evil infinite."[20] What is significant here, for my purposes, is that his analysis leads to an important insight: "Eve, then, does not stand for woman in the sense of 'second sex.' Every woman and every man are Adam; every man and every woman are Eve; every woman sins 'in' Adam; every man is seduced 'in' Eve."[21] This interchangeability of roles destroys a binary interpretation of Adam and Eve, such that Eve only represents women and Adam only represents men, with a resultant chain of implications. Rather, in each of them—Eve and Adam—we see revealed something that is true of all humans. When applied to the Mary and Jesus relationship, Ricoeur's insight will have enormous consequences.

19. Trible, *God and the Rhetoric,* 128.

20. Ricoeur, *The Symbolism of Evil,* 255.

21. Ricoeur, *The Symbolism of Evil,* 255. This understanding is also that of St. Paul, who saw Eve's seduction as having application to *all* believers, not just women. He wrote to the men and women of the church in Corinth, "But I am afraid that just as Eve was deceived by the serpent's cunning, your minds may somehow be led astray from your sincere and pure devotion to Christ" (2 Cor 11:3). Similarly, for Paul, Adam's disobedience was a model of *all* human disobedience, not just that of males (see Romans 5).

Among the many things that the Adamic myth reveals about evil, then, is that evil is both something to which we yield and something that we perpetuate by our freedom. For the human being, sin is an experience both of being seduced and of acting as an agent of seduction. Evil is always there before us and we, in turn, carry it forward. For Ricoeur, the serpent represents the evil that precedes us. Adam and Eve represent the two sides of the human experience of evil, sides that cannot be represented at one and the same time by a single figure. Thus, in Eve we see the seductive power and in Adam, the power to choose. However, the human experience for both men and women is captured in the couple. This means that the interpreter must resist making a one-to-one correspondence such that Eve stands for yielding and Adam stands for acting, nor such that Eve represents women and Adam, men. The truth of the human situation is revealed only by holding the two figures together and understanding the way in which the joint experience represents the whole.

Development of Dogma

The research lying behind official Catholic documents remains something of a mystery. We learned this lesson in 1988, when the bishops of the United States formulated a draft pastoral letter entitled, "Partners in the Mystery of Redemption." In addition to referencing previous papal teachings, the document had footnotes that cited the work of several women authors. For a number of reasons that draft was voted down. No subsequent version of the pastoral letter, which ultimately failed to be promulgated, had references to women authors, depending instead on official Church documents.

I mention this because it is impossible to know if the authors of the *Catechism of the Catholic Church* were influenced by the work of women scholars. The only women cited are female saints, and the most recent of them is Therese of Lisieux, who lived in the late nineteenth century. Yet, the *Catechism*, that most mainline of Catholic documents, teaches that

> Man and woman have been *created*, which is to say, *willed* by God: on the one hand, in perfect equality as human persons; on the other, in their respective beings as man and woman.[22]

In a later entry, it proclaims,

---

22. *Catechism of the Catholic Church*, art. 369.

Man and woman were made "for each other"—not that God left them half-made and incomplete: he created them to be a communion of persons, in which each can be "helpmate" to the other, for they are equal as persons . . . and complementary as masculine and feminine.[23]

It is certain that the 1988 Apostolic Letter of Pope John Paul II, "On the Dignity and Vocation of Women" (*Mulieris dignitatem*), exercised a great influence over what made its way into the *Catechism*. In the Letter, the Pope teaches that "both man and woman are human beings to an equal degree; both are created in God's image."[24] This point is reiterated thus: "The biblical text provides sufficient bases for recognizing the essential equality of man and woman from the point of view of their humanity."[25]

After centuries of theology in which the example of Eve was used to inculcate the created inferiority of women, this development is stunning. It also has important implications for the meaning of Mary as the new Eve.

Retrieving an Ancient Theology

A major feminist criticism of traditional Mariology is that the tradition insists that Mary is not a "type," showing forth what is true of all women. Rather, Mary is considered there as the great exception. According to these critics, this position pits Mary against other women and results in making other women feel hopelessly inferior to this one perfect specimen. Yet, the same theological tradition considered Eve the paradigm of all women, to the extent that Tertullian could address women of his time as Eve, railing at them for being continuing sources of temptation. In this, he was not alone.

It is not sufficient to criticize the inherited tradition, however. Where necessary, it must be corrected. If the male theological tradition made of Mary the great exception, elevating her above all others and preventing many women from identifying with her at all, then there is no reason why women, coming to the texts anew, should continue that line of thinking. In a renewed theology of Mary as the new Eve, it is possible to project a very different image of women and of the relationship between women and men. We are, after all, talking about redemption.

23. *Catechism of the Catholic Church*, art. 372.

24. John Paul II, "On the Dignity and Vocation of Women," art. 6.

25. John Paul II, "On the Dignity and Vocation of Women," art. 6.

If, as I believe, the artistry of Matthew, Luke, and John laid the groundwork for seeing Mary as the new Eve, a renewed understanding of the revelation of Genesis will have consequences for Marian theology. First of all, Eve is not to be understood as derived from and dependent on Adam. Rather, she comes from the hand of God, as did the man, and is subordinate only to that divine being—until the incursion of evil brings her under the rule of man. The new Eve imagery suggests another beginning: one where the effects of sin have been abrogated. Meditation on the Genesis text, then, can lead one to glimpse connections to the dogma of the immaculate conception, which holds that Mary, too, was created as a new being, free from the sad human history of sin.

As Eve, in the Genesis story, had her own relationship to God and was not obliged to relate to God through Adam, so might we now see Mary as a woman related directly to God and called to her own mission. If, in the mysterious interaction between mother and son later in life, she becomes in any sense Jesus' disciple, then her original interaction—as portrayed by the infancy narratives—is with God.[26]

Mary engages the heavenly messenger in the Lukan account, even as Eve discourses with the serpent. The young maid, Mary, does not consult her father or her betrothed before giving an answer, but replies in freedom and in faithfulness. Since Mary is addressed as "full of grace," one might say that grace precedes her choice in a way similar to the manner that evil preceded that of Eve in the creation myth. In this sense, Mary represents the human capacity to cooperate with the power of God, even being overshadowed by it to the point of being made fruitful. In this regard, she represents all of humanity, not just women.

Sexual stereotypes have blinded many interpreters to the active nature of Mary's role here. While Abraham, Paul, and Jesus himself are most often imaged as freely responding to a call, Mary's moment has been called "the annunciation," placing the emphasis on the angel's action and casting in shadows her own daring leap into the unknown. Informed by the insights of feminist scholars, believers can now see that, like Eve, Mary engages in a dialogue and, when satisfied, makes her own decision. She is receptive, yes,

---

26. Interpreters who operate from within the paradigm of Mary as first disciple do so based on the incident recorded in Mark 3:31–35, Matt 12:46–50, and Luke 8:19–21. See Bearsley, "Mary the Perfect Disciple," 461–504. This interpretation, in turn, affects their understanding of other episodes, such as the wedding feast of Cana, as shown in chapter 2.

but she is also an agent, giving her consent to a mission that will involve her whole being and her whole life.

The Matthean account also makes clear that Joseph has not been consulted or even informed. Mary is off-stage here, but the structure of the narrative suggests one who has made her commitment and waits in trust for God to work things out.

This same waiting in trust is even more evident in the Johannine account of the wedding feast. There, Mary anticipates a crisis, points it out to Jesus, refuses to be put off by his sharp response, moves in her own way to put things in motion for a resolution, and trusts that the one she has raised will act according to his upbringing. The Cana narrative shows a woman and a man cooperating to bring about a rescue of the situation, reversing the interaction of the original man and woman who plunged the world into a time of exile.

As the new Eve, Mary is a partner to Jesus. She is a "helpmate," but no less so than he is. Tina Beattie captures the power of this with her words:

> Mary was the new woman just as Jesus was the new man. They both belong within the new world that was initiated at the Annunciation and celebrated in the *Magnificat*, but that will only be fulfilled at the end of time. As creatures and spirits of the new world, Mary and Jesus lived as a promise and a beacon to all who would follow. They lived not in Paradise nor in Eden but in this temporal, fallen world; and therefore, they were buffeted and tormented by the injustices of life, but they were not part of the sinful order of domination, and nothing in their lives lends any justification to those who would perpetuate the old hierarchies between men and women.[27]

We saw the graced imagination go to work on the possibilities here in a variety of ways as devotion to Mary, public and private, continued to develop in the Christian community. These texts also inspired creative works that drew out the significance of Mary's life, her relationship with God, and her companionship with Jesus. One can imagine that this line of development might have continued, had it not been for the Protestant Reformation.

27. Beattie, *Rediscovering Mary*, 90.

CHAPTER 8

Conclusion
The Passion of Mary
and Mothering the Church

Introduction

PREVIOUS CHAPTERS HAVE GIVEN glimpses of a tradition that considers Mary a companion to Jesus, a woman who, like him, is human to the utmost. Elements of this tradition shone through in John's account of the wedding feast at Cana. They reappear in patristic interpretations of Mary as the new Eve and in the development of feasts and devotions in which parallel events in the lives of Jesus and Mary are celebrated. There are hints in the immaculate conception of Mary, which affirms her total freedom from sin and suggests a divine election going back to creation. The assumption is the capstone, professing that Mary was taken up, body and soul, to reign with Jesus the Christ in the heavenly realm. These glimmers are there despite the fact that Christology was developed first, and the revelation about Mary was read within the lens of that Christology.

The New Testament begins Mary's story with her prophetic call and commission. After greeting her with a salutation—"The Lord is with you"[1]—that is resonant with overtones of another divine appeal,[2] an angel delivers a message that is also an invitation: "And now, you will conceive in your womb and bear a son, and you will name him Jesus." The summons

1. Luke 1:28.
2. Judg 6:12.

requires that she give her body—indeed, her whole being—over to the designs of God. It will change the direction of her life and, accepted, will commit her to a path shrouded in darkness and fraught with danger. Is it any wonder, then, that artists often include in annunciation scenes representations or suggestions of a cross?[3]

It is difficult to tell from the biblical text when the revelation to Joseph occurred. What we can know is that once he has accepted the mysterious nature of Mary's pregnancy and she has been spared being "dismissed quietly,"[4] the two unite in bringing the child to birth, protecting him from danger and doing for him according to the Law. Circumstances deprive them of a bed for their newborn, making it necessary to lay the child in a manger: a food trough for animals. It is there that shepherds and magi find him. The image of the manger anticipates the way in which the child will give himself to his followers forever. Painters seem to delight in playing with its shape and meaning, at times in order to anticipate death. Ghirlandaio, for instance, makes of the manger a sarcophagus in his famous painting, "The Adoration of the Shepherds." There is nothing in the biblical narrative to indicate that Mary is not at home with both workers in the fields and wise men from afar, as will her child be so at ease. Nor is there any record of her objecting when Joseph, alerted in a dream to impending danger to the newborn, moves them all to a foreign land. We hear nothing from her as well when a dream directs her husband to return to their home. If the escape from Herod's murderous intent was not enough to alert the mother to the troubles of the son, Simeon's words to her at the time of his being presented in the temple certainly drive home the realization: "This child is destined for the falling and the rising of many in Israel, and to be a sign that will be opposed so that the inner thoughts of many will be revealed; and a sword will pierce your own soul, too."[5] Mary's son's being the cause of the deaths of many other children was surely one of the ways in which her soul was pierced. There will be others.

---

3. Perhaps the clearest example is in Robert Campin's *Annunciation Triptych*. The central panel, which depicts the angel's appearance to Mary, shows all windows with a cross within and a small figure of a baby flying toward Mary on a stream of light, carrying a cross. See Dupré, *Full of Grace*, 122–23.

4. Matt 1:19.

5. Luke 2:34–35.

Still, as all parents must, Mary is to know the pain of separation as Jesus comes under the influence of another.[6] Having kept company with John the Baptist, Jesus embarks on a life that is unconventional and worrisome; "danger threatens from the Jewish authorities and from the hated occupying power of the Romans."[7] Perhaps that is why his mother, with other members of the family, goes in search of him. This time, the response they receive is not in the form of puzzling questions, but in an astonishing expansion of the meaning of family. Jesus lets it be known that he considers anyone who does the will of God to be his "brother and sister and mother."[8] It is an episode that foreshadows their final meeting when Jesus will commission the one he calls "woman," in full confidence that she has embraced this understanding as her own. Of the time in between, we know little. Yet, the experiences of learning to accept the surprises and the

6. I refer here only to Mary because there is no mention of Joseph in any texts concerning interaction between the adult Jesus and his family.

7. Ben-Chorin, "A Jewish View of the Mother of Jesus," cited in Johnson, *Truly Our Sister*, 220.

8. Mark 3:35. While many interpreters have considered this statement tantamount to a rejection of family ties, I see it as evidence of the preciousness of family ties. Jesus does not say, "I have no sister or brother or mother." Rather, he embraces as family those who, like him, seek to do God's will.

reversals of watching one's child mature can provide us with insight into Mary's struggles as mother and as servant of God.

Mary is the human being called to bear divine-human life and to take responsibility for bringing this life to maturity under difficult human conditions. In accepting this mission, she herself is changed. Charlene Spretnak dares to call it an "ontological change," an idea that she explains thus: "She occupies a unique type of being that did not exist before. Rather than excluding the biblical narrative, this orientation is built on Mary's unique and *elemental* role in the Incarnation and the ministry of Christ."[9] It was in her body that the material link between divinity and humanity took shape and came to fruition. She is and ever will be the matrix: in the words of Spretnak, "she who melds the human and the cosmological."[10] It is initially because of her role in the great mystery of the incarnation that later generations will expand the scope of their understanding and their praise of this daughter of God about whom the Bible reveals so much while saying so little. The first step was to call her "Mother of God."

Mary's mission was carried out, for the most part, in the family and, later, within the community of Christ's followers. Jesus' mission took him on the road, to far flung towns where he encountered and changed people previously unknown to him.

The Passion of Mary

Let us now move forward in our study of the mystery of Mary by reflecting on a dimension of the paschal mystery: the passion of Mary. We do so, not because Mary's portion of suffering is more appropriate for women, but because it can teach us something true about the whole human experience, even as does the passion of Jesus. The truth of Mary's paradigm has been left in the shadows. It is time to bring it into the light.

British child psychologist D. W. Winnicott originated an interesting term for the kind of space that encourages a child's growth: he terms it the "holding" environment.[11] Sally Cunneen claims that the most widespread cultural and artistic symbol of the holding environment is the mother's

9. Spretnak, *Missing Mary*, 4.

10. Spretnak, *Missing Mary*, 90.

11. See a reference to this term in Castelloe, "A Holding Environment & Beyond 9/11."

lap.[12] More often than is commonly realized, the great shrines to Mary were built on sites previously dedicated to a mother-goddess. These were places of preservation for thrones on which a goddess sat, often with a child on her lap. Cunneen maintains, for example, that the depiction of Mary at Chartres is based on the earlier image of Isis holding her son Horus so. "In this way," she writes,

> Mary brings the protective, nurturing function of the divine in prehistoric Pagan times into the heart of Christian tradition. . . . Mary's lap is one of the most consistent symbols of a holding environment in human history, . . . the symbol . . . speaks of the continuity of the human desire for secure mothering: natural, cultural, and spiritual.[13]

Meeting the Beloved on the Way of the Cross

No specific text from Scripture presents this scene. Instead, we rely on the devotional memory of the community of faith, a memory that is enshrined in the Stations of the Cross: the encounter between Mary and Jesus on the *Via Dolorosa*. Perhaps, like the story of the temptations of Jesus itself, this "station" is meant to sum up a much longer period of time, a period in which Mary struggled with her own temptations as she watched her son become more and more vulnerable, more and more determined to risk it all in the face of the overwhelming powers of temple and state.

Once, when my niece Sacha[14] was about five years old, she said to me: "Aunt Mary Ann, how come Jesus didn't just run away if he knew they were coming to get him?" From the heart of a child comes the question of a lifetime.

Drive the question closer to home. How come the Maryknoll women did not leave El Salvador?[15] How come the Precious Blood sisters did not leave Liberia?[16] Why did the Franciscans not move their motherhouse when the neighborhood so clearly was changing and their security less and

12. Cunneen, *Mother Church*, 57–58.

13. Cunneen, *Mother Church*, 57–58.

14. As an adult, Sacha Ludwig worked at the Mount Saint Agnes Theological Center for Women in Baltimore.

15. Bonner, "The Diplomat and the Killer" (1 Dec. 1980).

16. "Liberia Martyrs" (20 Oct. 1992).

less assured? Why is a simple fireman from Rhode Island going into Bosnia when everyone else is fleeing?[17] Why did the first responders to the terror on September 11 go toward the disaster rather than run from it?[18]

Standing with Mary on the way of the cross we find ourselves at the epicenter of the paschal mystery. The Sacred Scriptures offer us no help here; they do not tell us that they met; or what, if anything, Mary said to Jesus as she heard reports of his teaching and acting in ways that would surely lead to his death. In all four Gospels: silence. There is nothing but silence about Mary until, as in John's Gospel, it is all but over.

The Death of the Beloved Other

"The decisive encounter with death is the death of a being I love."[19] From this statement, the author, Paul Ricoeur, goes on to fill in the contours of this encounter:

> Here death is really sensed as my end: irreparable. Death, in second person, is the true illustration of death as the law of the species. And this end has repercussions in me as the end of communication: The dead is one who no longer responds. He is absent, vanished. For this radical experience, we need neither an elaborate colorful image of agony nor the equivalent spectacle of a corpse, nor funeral rites. It spreads out in the sheer absence, which is only in the hearts, and it is this silence which lends gravity to the final agony, which lends the corpse its desolation . . . and grief to funeral rites which it makes a solemn farewell. . . . Love suffers precisely because one is gone and the other remains: each [person] dies alone and each is left alone on the shore.[20]

Dare we think about what Mary must have experienced in the death of Jesus? If there was an understanding between Jesus and Mary that mirrored their relationship to God in prayer, surely for her this must have been the dark night of the soul.

Generations of believers have marveled at the faith of Abraham as demonstrated in his readiness to sacrifice his son at God's command. Subsequent musings have created a whole tradition of interpretation of

17. "R.I. firefighter seeks help for peers in Sarajevo" (22 Feb. 1993).

18. History.com, "9/11 Timeline" (11 Sept. 2010).

19. Ricoeur, "Consent and Necessity," 460.

20. Ricoeur, "Consent and Necessity," 460.

the sacrifice of Isaac, the only-begotten son. What prevents us from seeing in the figure of Mary one who surpasses Abraham, who sacrifices indeed? Do we diminish her offering because we imagine that she could not have stopped it, could not have made it be otherwise? Or, is it that one who only conceives the son is considered less an actor in the drama? What is Mary's role in Jesus' offering of himself to God?

Mary Cleophas Costello, RSM, a beloved president of Mount Saint Agnes College, used to say that the etchings of Rembrandt on the Abraham/Isaac story constituted a marvelous sustained meditation on the nature of sacrifice. In the earliest of the series, Abraham is standing at a distance from Isaac and is about to hurl something at his son. In the last, Abraham enfolds Isaac with one arm while, with the other, he raises the instrument of sacrifice. I would suggest that something similar takes place in the Christian imagination.

In the earliest of the accounts of the passion, the women are standing afar, silent witnesses to the horror of what is unfolding. The mother of Jesus is not identified as one of the women. By the time John's Gospel is written, however, the mother of Jesus is pictured standing beneath the cross with the disciple whom Jesus loved. Later, visual artists went to work on the scene, further interpreting the meaning of Mary's passion. And in what has surely become the most loved of all the artistic renditions, the *Pietà*, the broken body of the Christ is returned to the holding environment, to the lap of the mother, to be joined once more with her capacious body and given forth to the world as sacrificed for the sins of all.

Much has been made by contemporary theologians of Jesus' rejection of any claim on Mary's part to a special role in his life because of her physical motherhood. They say that Jesus clearly rejected this in the passage where he says, "My mother and my brothers are those who hear the word of God and do it."[21] But there are *four* Gospels. Surely this quotation from the early years of his public ministry must be heard as completed by the words: "Woman, here is your son" and to the disciple whom he loved, "Here is your mother."[22] As Abraham was given back his son and with the son his fatherhood, Mary is given back a son and with him, her motherhood. Jesus does not say, "Brother, behold your sister." He says, "Here is your mother."

It was with growing amazement that I re-read the commentaries, commentaries I have read a dozen times before. In one way or another, they all say that John took Mary home to take care of her. Given the meditations in which we have been engaged, I think that is entirely backwards. I think that John took Mary to "his own," meaning to his own circle, so that she could be to them what she had been to Jesus: the shaping presence in

21. Luke 8:21.

22. John 19:26–27.

their lives. She mothered the new community as it struggled through its own time of maturation into the body of Christ. It is no accident that the Johannine community is marked by a spirit of mutual love or that scholars are now discovering to their wonderment that there are no gender roles in this community of faith.[23]

Conclusion

As we bring this examination of the original grace that is Mary's and this reflection on her passion to a close, let us be drawn deeply into the outline of her paschal mystery. She, who was warned of the cost of motherhood at the presentation in the temple, came to know the risks of it as she hauled her son away from the same temple and away from the patterns of behavior he was imitating there. She, who heard him extend the language of family ties to all those willing to hear and do the word of God, watched as that new family unraveled before the power and force of religious and state authority. She watched as he was abandoned and left to walk the way of the cross and die the ignominious death of a convicted criminal. Whatever was her dark night, our faith tells us that she came through it, as did her son. Unlike the mythical Adam and Eve, the new woman and the new man do not turn against each other and away from God. Each bears the allotted portion of human suffering in radical faithfulness.

Perhaps it is not too much to suggest that, in our time, women of the Church are called to a similar passion. We must know what mothering a renewed Church will cost, what risks must be taken to resist and correct models of behavior that do not befit the servants of God. We must be prepared to be told that we have misunderstood what it means to be women or mothers or sisters. We must even watch the body of Christ torn asunder by authorities bent on preserving exterior forms. Let us pray for the grace to stand near, to know our summons when it comes, and to receive the broken body of Christ's Church into loving laps of mercy. Meanwhile, let us not cease from longing for the new life that rises from such darkness and such death.

23. Anderson, "The Johannine Community."

Bibliography

Abbott, Walter M., SJ, ed. *The Documents of Vatican II*. Translated by Joseph Gallagher. New York: Herder and Herder, 1966.

Anderson, Janice Capel, and Stephen D. Moore, eds. *Mark and Method: New Approaches in Biblical Studies*. Minneapolis: Fortress, 1992.

Anderson, Paul. "The Johannine Community." In *Bible Odyssey*. https://www.bibleodyssey.org/en/people/related-articles/johannine-community.

Aquinas, Thomas. *Summa Theologiae III*. Christian Classics. Notre Dame, IN: Ave Maria, 1981.

Athans, Mary Christine, BVM. *In Quest of the Jewish Mary: The Mother of Jesus in History, Theology, and Spirituality*. Maryknoll, NY: Orbis, 2013.

Atkins, Kim. "Paul Ricoeur (1913–2005)." In *Internet Encyclopedia of Philosophy*. https://www.iep.utm.edu/ricoeur.

Augustine of Hippo. "*Sermo 52 de Trinitate*." https://www.augustinus.it/latino/discorsi/discorso_064_testo.htm.

Baker, Robert, and Barbara Budde, eds. *A Sourcebook about Mary*. Chicago: Liturgy Training, 2002.

Balasuriya, Tissa. *Mary and Human Liberation: The Story and the Text*. Norcross, GA: Trinity, 1997.

Bateson, Mary Catherine. *Composing a Life*. New York: Grove, 2001.

Bearsley, Patrick J., SM. "Mary the Perfect Disciple: A Paradigm of Mariology." *Theological Studies* 41.3 (1980) 461–504.

Beattie, Tina. *God's Mother, Eve's Advocate*. New York: Continuum, 2002.

———. *Rediscovering Mary: Insights from the Gospels*. Chicago: Triumph, 1995.

———. "'Women full and overflowing with grace': The Virgin Mary and the Contemporary Church." *The Way*. https://www.theway.org.uk/back/s093Beattie.pdf

Beauduin, Lambert, OSB. *Give Us This Day, Daily Prayer for Today's Catholic*, Jan. 2014. Collegeville, MN: Liturgical, 2014.

Beaumont, Madeleine, and Mary Misrahi, eds. *Days of the Lord. Volume 7: Solemnities and Feasts*. Collegeville, MN: Liturgical, 1994.

Beckett, Wendy. *Sister Wendy's Nativity*. New York: HarperCollins, 1998.

Bednar, Gerald J. *Faith as Imagination*. New York: Sheed and Ward, 1996.

Bibliography

Ben-Chorin, Schalom. "A Jewish View of the Mother of Jesus." In *Mary in the Churches*, edited by Hans Küng and Jürgen Moltmann, 12–24. Edinburgh: T. & T. Clark, 1983.

Benedict XVI. "Assumption Day Address." http://www.asianews.it/news-en/Jesus,-the-new-Adam,-and-Mary,-the-new-Eve,-finally-defeat-the-enemy,-pope-says-on-Assumption-Day-22366.html.

———. "Pope's Homily on Solemnity of the Assumption," Castel Gandolfo, Italy; 16 Aug. 2012. https://zenit.org/articles/pope-s-homily-on-solemnity-of-the-assumption/

Berlin, Adele. *Poetics and Interpretation of Biblical Narrative*. University Park, PA: Penn State University Press, 1994.

Bodkin, Thomas. "The Assumption in Art." *Furrow* 1.10 (1950).

Bonner, Raymond. "The Diplomat and the Killer (1 Dec. 1980)." *Atlantic*, 11 Feb. 2016.

Boss, Sarah Jane. "The Cosmos in Her Womb. " *Tablet*, 1 Jan. 2005.

———. *Empress and Handmaid: On Nature and Gender in the Cult of the Virgin Mary*. London: Cassell, 2000.

———, ed. *Mary: The Complete Resource*. Oxford: Oxford University Press, 2007.

Botticelli, Sandro. "The Annunciation." https://fineartamerica.com/featured/the-annunciation-botticelli.html.

———. "Cestello Annunciation" (Tempera on panel, 1489–1490). In the Uffizi, Florence, Italy.

Braaten, Carl E., and Robert W. Jenson, eds. *Mary, Mother of God*. Grand Rapids: Eerdmans, 2004.

Bradley, Ben. "'Shakespeare's Mighty Sorority: Women of Will' at the Gym at Judson Memorial Church." *The New York Times*, 3 Feb. 2013.

Brown, Raymond E. *The Birth of the Messiah: A Commentary on the Infancy Narratives in the Gospels of Matthew and Luke*. New York: Doubleday, 1977.

———. *The Birth of the Messiah*. Updated ed. New Haven, CT: Yale University Press, 1999.

Brown, Raymond E., et al., eds. *Mary in the New Testament*. Mahwah, NJ: Paulist, 1978.

Buonarroti, Michelangelo. *Pietà* (marble, 1498–99). In St. Peter's Basilica at the Vatican.

Burghardt, Walter J., SJ. "The Testimony of the Patristic Age Concerning Mary's Death." *Woodstock Papers*, No. 2. Mahwah, NJ: Newman/Paulist, 1957.

Burnett, Fred W. "Characterization and Reader Construction of Characters in the Gospels." *Semeia* 63. *Characterization in Biblical Literature*, edited by Elizabeth Struthers Malbon and Adele Berlin (1993) 3–28.

Byassee, Jason. "Protestants and Marian Devotion: What about Mary?" *The Christian Century*, 14 Dec. 2014.

Canan, Janine, ed. *She Rises Like the Sun*. Toronto: Crossing, 1989.

Castelloe, Molly S. "A Holding Environment & Beyond 9/11." *Psychology Today*, 11 Sept. 2010.

Castillo, Ana, ed. *Goddess of the Americas: Writings on the Virgin of Guadalupe*. New York: Riverhead, 1996.

Catechism of the Catholic Church. United States Catholic Conference. Vatican: Libreria Editrice Vaticana, 1994/Liguori, MO: Liguori, 1994.

Clapton, Eric, and Stephen Bishop. "Holy Mother." BMG Rights Management, Downtown Music Publishing, Warner Chappell Music, Inc., 1986.

Clark, Anne L. "The Priesthood of the Virgin Mary: Gender Trouble in the Twelfth Century." *Journal of Feminist Studies in Religion* 18.1 (2002) 5–24.

Bibliography

Coles, Katharine. "Annunciation." Jan. 2019. https://www.patheos.com/blogs/goodletters/2015/12/poetry-Friday-annunciation-by-katerine-coles/.

Conway, Ann. "The Rosary." *Image* issue 62. https://imagejournal.org/article/the-rosary/

Conway, Colleen M. *Men and Women in the Fourth Gospel: Gender and Johannine Characterization*. Atlanta: SBL, 1999.

Cummings, Owen. F. "Understanding the Immaculate Conception." *Furrow* 30.12 (1979) 767–71.

Cunneen, Sally. *In Search of Mary: The Woman and the Symbol*. New York: Ballantine, 1996.

———. *Mother Church: What the Experience of Women Is Teaching Her*. Mahwah, NJ: Paulist, 1991.

Daly, Mary. *The Church and the Second Sex*. Boston: Beacon, 1986.

Darr, John A. *On Character Building: The Reader and the Rhetoric of Characterization in Luke-Acts*. Louisville, KY: Westminster John Knox, 1992.

Davis, Ellen. "Reading the Song Iconographically." In *Scrolls of Love: Ruth and the Song of Songs*, edited by Peter S. Hawkins and Lesleigh Cushing Stahlberg, 172–84. New York: Fordham University Press, 2006.

DeConick, April D. *Holy Misogyny: Why the Sex and Gender Conflicts in the Early Church Still Matter*. New York: Continuum, 2011.

deKoninck, Charles. "The Immaculate Conception and the Divine Motherhood, Assumption and Coredemption." In *The Dogma of the Immaculate Conception, History and Significance*, edited by Edward D. O'Connor, CSC, 363–412. Notre Dame, IN: University of Notre Dame Press, 1958.

Diekmann, Godfrey, OSB. *Come, Let Us Worship*. Abingdon, UK: Helicon, 1961.

Donahey, Mary. "Mary, Mirror of Justice: A Challenge for the Church to Reflect Justice." In *Mary According to Women*, edited by Carol Frances Jergen, BVM, 71–87. New York: Sheed and Ward, 1985.

Donahue, John R., SJ. "The Literary Turn and New Testament Theology." *The Journal of Religion* 76.2 (1996) 250–75.

———. "Things Old and Things New in Biblical Interpretation." *The Way Supplement* 72 (1991) 20–31.

Duffy, Margaret. "Iconography of the Resurrection—Christ Appears to His Mother." *Ad Imaginem Dei*. (2011, 2017). http://imaginemdei.blogspot.com/2011/06/iconography-of-resurrection-christ.html.

Dupré, Judith. *Full of Grace: Encountering Mary in Faith, Art, and Life*. New York: Random, 2010.

Ebertshauser, Caroline H., et al., eds. *Mary: Art, Culture, and Religion through the Ages*. Translated by Peter Heinegg. New York: Crossroad, 1998.

Encyclopedia Britannica, eds. *Encylopaedia Britannica*, "Saint Justin Martyr, Christian Apologist."

———. "Second Vatican Council: Roman Catholic History (1962–1965)."

Estés, Clarissa Pinkola. "Guadalupe: The Path of the Broken Heart." In *Goddess of the Americas: Writings on the Virgin of Guadalupe*, edited by Ana Castillo. New York: Riverhead, 1997.

———. *Untie the Strong Woman: Blessed Mother's Immaculate Love for the Wild Soul*. Louisville: Sounds True, 2011.

Fein, Susanna Greer, ed. "Art. 60, Stond wel, moder, under rode." In *The Complete Harley 2253 Manuscript*, Vol. 2, 2014. https://d.lib.rochester.edu/camelot/text/fein-harley2253-volume-2-article-60.

FitzGerald, Kyriaki Karidoyanes. "Mary the *Theotokos* and the Call to Holiness." In *Mary, Mother of God*, edited by Carl E. Braaten and Robert W. Jenson, 80–99. Grand Rapids: Eerdmans, 2004.

Fra Angelico. "The Annunciatory Angel and the Virgin Annunciate" (*Parma tabernacle*, tempera on panel). In *Fra Angelico for the Metropolitan Museum of Art*, by Laurence Kanter and Pia Palladino, 108. New Haven, CT: Yale University Press, 2005.

Fransen, P. "In Memorium: Felix Malmberg." 2 Jan. 2013. https://www.tandfonline.com/doi/abs/10.1080/00062278.1979.10596787.

Galland, China. *Longing for Darkness: Tara and the Black Madonna. A Ten-Year Journey.* London: Penguin, 1990.

Gaventa, Beverly Roberts, and Cynthia L. Rigby, eds. *Blessed One: Protestant Perspectives on Mary.* Louisville, KY: Westminster John Knox, 2002.

Gebara, Ivone, and Maria Clara Bingemer. *Mary, Mother of God, Mother of the Poor.* Maryknoll, NY: Orbis, 1996.

Ghirlandaio, Domenico. "The Adoration of the Shepherds." https://www.bing.com/images/search?q=ghirlandaio+paintings&view=detailv2&id=76504B72F2651441DD5CCD31C3CAE982DF73FF7E&selectedindex=0&thid=JN.FUYtBgRR7dE5NdbNGG5H%2Bw&ajaxhist=0&exph=0&expw=0&vt=0.

Graef, Hilda. *Mary: A History of Doctrine and Devotion.* Notre Dame: Ave Maria, 2009.

Grey, Mary. "Reclaiming Mary: A Task for Feminist Theology." *The Way* 29.4 (1989) 334–40.

Griffin, Patty. "Mary." https://www.google.com/search?client=avast&q=Mary+you%27re+covered+in+roses%2C+you%27re+covered+in+ashes+You%27re+covered+in+rain.

Guéranger, Prosper, OSB. *The Liturgical Year: Volume 1—Advent.* Fitzwilliam, NH: Loreto, 2013.

Guite, Malcolm. *Faith, Hope and Poetry.* Abingdon, UK: Routledge, 2017.

Hayes, Richard B. *Reading Backwards: Figural Christology and the Fourfold Gospel Witness.* Waco, TX: Baylor University Press, 2014.

Heal, Bridget. "Images of the Virgin Mary and Marian Devotion in Protestant Nuremberg." In *Religion and Superstition in Reformation Europe,* edited by Helen Parish and William G. Naphy, 25–46. Manchester, UK: Manchester University Press, 2002.

Heaney, Seamus. "In Gallarus Oratory." In *Door into the Dark.* London: Faber and Faber, 1969.

History.com, eds. "9/11 Timeline." *History.* A&E Television Networks, 21 Jun. 2011.

Holy Bible: The New Revised Standard Version with Apocrypha. Nashville: Thomas Nelson, 1989.

Hornik, Heidi J., and Mikeal C. Parsons. *Illumination Luke: The Infancy Narrative in Italian Renaissance Painting.* New York: Trinity, 2003.

Hudgins, Andrew. "The Cestello Annunciation." In *Upholding Mystery: An Anthology of Contemporary Christian Poetry,* edited by David Impastato. New York: Oxford University Press, 1997.

Hughes, Kathleen, RSCJ. *The Monk's Tale: A Biography of Godfrey Diekmann, OSB.* Collegeville, MN: Liturgical, 1991.

Bibliography

Impastato, David, ed. *An Anthology of Contemporary Christian Poetry*. New York: Oxford University Press, 1997.

International Marian Research Institute, eds. *All About Mary: Encyclopedia of Information on Mary, the Mother of Jesus Christ*. https://udayton.edu/imri/mary/index.php.

Irenaeus of Lyons. "The Analogy of Eve and the Theotokos." In *Against Heresies*, Book III ch. 22.

Jergen, Carol Frances, BVM, ed. *Mary According to Women*. Kansas City: Leaven, 1985.

Jillions, John. "Fr. Thomas Hopko: Church Administration as Service to God." *Orthodox Church in America*, 23 Aug. 2013.

John Paul II. Apostolic Letter, "On the Dignity and Vocation of Women" (*Mulieris dignitatem*), 1994. http://w2.vatican.va/content/john-paul-ii/en/apost letters/1994/ documents.

———. "*Redemptor hominis*." *Origins* 8.40 (1979).

Johnson, Elizabeth A., CSJ. *Dangerous Memories: A Mosaic of Mary in Scripture*. New York: Continuum, 2006.

———. *Friends of God and Prophets: A Feminist Theological Reading of the Communion of Saints*. New York: Continuum, 1998.

———. "The Marian Tradition and the Reality of Women." *Horizons* 12.1 (1985) 116–35.

———. *Truly Our Sister: A Theology of Mary in the Communion of Saints*. New York: Continuum, 2003.

Jones, Judith Kaye. *The Women in the Gospel of John: The Divine Feminine*. Atlanta: Chalice, 2008.

Joseph, Aimee. "The View from the Pew: The Delicate Balance between Simple and Sensory Worship." 15 Sept. 2015. https://aimeejoseph.blog/page/36/?ref=spelling.

Jung, C. G. "Answer to Job." In *Psychology and Religion: West and East*, 2nd ed. *Collected Works of C. G. Jung*, Vol. 11; Bollingen Series XX. Translated by R. F. C. Hull. Princeton: Princeton University Press, 1969.

Kaminski, Phyllis H. "What the Daughter Knows: Re-tinking Women's Religious Experience with and against Luce Irigary." In *Encountering Transcendence: Contributions to a Theology of Christian Religious Experience*, edited by Lieven Boeve, et al., 57–82. Dudley, MA: Peeters, 2005.

Kaminsky, Ilya, and Katherine Tower, eds. *A God in the House: Poets Talk about Faith*. North Adams, MA: Tupelo, 2012.

Kanter, Laurence, and Pia Palladino. "The Annunciatory Angel and The Virgin Annunciate." In *Fra Angelico for The Metropolitan Museum of Art*, 108. New Haven, CT: Yale University Press, 2005.

Kidd, Sue Monk. *The Secret Life of Bees*. New York: Viking, 2002.

Kidd, Sue Monk, and Ann Kidd Taylor. *Traveling with Pomegranates: A Mother-Daughter Story*. New York: Viking, 2009.

Kristeva, Julia. "Stabat Mater." Translated by Arthur Goldhammer. In "The Female Body in Western Culture: Semiotic Perspectives." *Poetics Today* 6.1/2 (1985) 133–52.

Kuhrt, Jon. "'Proper Confidence in the Gospel': The Theology of Lesslie Newbigin." *Fulcrum*, 23 Dec. 2009.

Küng, Hans. *The Council in Action: Theological Reflections on the Second Vatican Council*. Translated by Cecily Hastings. London: Sheed and Ward, 1963.

Leclercq, Jean, OSB. *The Love of Learning and the Desire for God: A Study of Monastic Culture*. New York: Fordham University Press, 1982.

Bibliography

Levering, Matthew. *Mary's Bodily Assumption*. Notre Dame, IN: University of Notre Dame Press, 2015.

Levine, Amy-Jill, with Maria Mayo Robbins, eds. *A Feminist Companion to Mariology: Feminist Companion to the New Testament and Early Christian Writings*. London: T. & T. Clark, 2005.

"Liberia Martyrs. 20 Oct. 1992." *Adorers of the Blood of Christ*. https://adorers.org/asc-liberia-martyrs/.

Linsenmayer, Mark. "Paul Ricoeur on the 'Second Naiveté.'" The Partially Examined Life blog (29 Mar. 2015). https://partiallyexaminedlife.com/2015/03/29/ricoeur-on-the-second-naivete/.

Litany of Loreto. https://www.ewtn.com/faith/teachings/maryd6f.htm.

The Little Office of the Blessed Virgin Mary. 1915. Reprint, New York: Benziger Brothers, 1945.

Livings, Jack. "Tobias Wolff, The Art of Fiction, No. 183." *The Paris Review* no. 171 (2004). https://www.theparisreview.org/interviews/5391/the-art-of-fiction-no-183-tobias-wolff.

Lotto, Lorenzo. "Annunciation." http://www.lorenzolottomarche.it/en/annunciazione-15271529/.

Lynch, William F., SJ. *Images of Faith: An Exploration of the Ironic Imagination*. Notre Dame, IN: University of Notre Dame Press, 1973.

Maeckelberghe, Els. *Desperately Seeking Mary: A Feminist Appropriation of a Traditional Religious Symbol*. Kamden, Netherlands: Kok Pharos, 1994.

Malbon, Elizabeth Struthers, and Adele Berlin, eds. *Semeia* 63. *Characterization in Biblical Literature*. Atlanta: SBL, 1993.

Malbon, Elizabeth Struthers. "Narrative Criticism: How Does the Story Mean?" In *Mark and Method: New Approaches in Biblical Studies*, edited by Janice Capel Anderson and Stephen D. Moore, 29–58. Minneapolis: Fortress, 1992.

Martínez, Rubén. "The Undocumented Virgin." In *Goddess of the Americas: Writings on the Virgin of Guadalupe*, edited by Ana Castillo. New York: Riverhead, 1996.

Maunder, Chris. "Mary in the New Testament and Apocrypha." In *Mary: The Complete Resource*, edited by Sarah Jane Boss, 11–49. Oxford: Oxford University Press, 2007.

McEnroy, Carmel, RSM. *Guests in Their Own House: The Women of Vatican II*. Eugene, OR: Wipf & Stock, 2011.

Meissen, Randall, L. C. "A Mother's Hand Guided the Bullets: John Paul II Forgiving a Would-Be Assassin." *Catholic Online*, 27 Apr. 2011.

Miravalle, Mark I. *Mary: Coredemptrix, Mediatrix, Advocate*. Goleta, CA: Queenship, 1993.

Mitchell, Nathan. *The Mystery of the Rosary: Marian Devotion and the Reinvention of Catholicism*. New York: New York University Press, 2009.

Newbigin, Lesslie. *The Other Side of 1984: Questions for the Churches*. Geneva: World Council of Churches, 1990.

New Catholic Encyclopedia, eds. "Sanctoral Cycle." *Encyclopedia.com*. 2003.

O'Carroll, Michael, ed. "*Sub Tuum*." In *Theotokos: A Theological Encyclopedia of the Blessed Virgin Mary*. Collegeville, MN: Liturgical, 1982.

O'Connor, Edward D., CSC. "Modern Theories of Original Sin, and the Dogma of the Immaculate Conception." *Marian Studies* 20.1 (1969) 112–36.

O'Neill, Mary Aquin, RSM. "An Apostleship of Equals." *Journal of the Mercy Association in Scripture and Theology* 3.3 (1993) 8–11.

Bibliography

————. "Current Theology: Toward A Renewed Anthropology." *Theological Studies* 36.4 (1975) 725–46.

————. "Female Embodiment and the Incarnation." In *Themes in Feminist Theology for the New Millennium,* Vol. 1, edited by Francis Eigo, 35–66. Villanova, PA: Villanova University Press, 2002.

————. "Feminist Theology: The Heart of the Matter." In *Full of Hope: Critical Social Perspectives on Theology,* edited by Magdala Thompson, 1–19. Mahwah, NJ: Paulist, 2003.

————. "Imagine Being Human: An Anthropology of Mutuality." In *Miriam's Song II as Patriarchy: A Feminist Critique,* 11–14. West Hyattsville, MD: Priests for Equality, 1988.

————. "The Marian Principle: Women in the Roman Catholic Church." In *Creating a Home: Benchmarks for Church Leadership Roles for Women,* edited by Jeanean D. Merkel. Silver Spring, MD: Leadership Conference of Women Religious, Special Report, 1996.

————. "The Mystery of Being Human Together." In *Freeing Theology: The Essentials of Theology* in *Feminist Perspective,* edited by Catherine Mowry LaCugna, 139–60. San Francisco: Harper & Row, 1993.

————. "The Nature of Women and the Method of Theology." *Theological Studies* 56.4 (1995) 730–42.

————. "Revealing Imagination: A Study of Paul Ricoeur." PhD diss., Vanderbilt University, 1981.

Orsi, Robert Anthony. *Madonna of 115th Street: Faith and Community in Italian Harlem— 1880–1950.* New Haven, CT: Yale University Press, 1985.

————. "She Came, She Saw, She Conquered." *Commonweal* 124.5 (1997).

Ostriker, Alicia. "God the Mother." In *A God in the House: Poets Talk about Faith,* edited by Ilya Kaminsky and Katherine Tower. North Adams, MA: Tupelo, 2012.

Palmer, Paul F., SJ. *Mary in the Documents of the Church.* Mahwah, NJ: Newman/Paulist, 1952.

Parish, Helen, and William G. Naphy, eds. *Religion and Superstition in Reformation Europe.* Manchester, UK: Manchester University Press, 2002.

Parsch, Pius. *The Church's Year of Grace,* Vol. 5. Collegeville, MN: Liturgical, 1962.

Paul VI, *"Marialis Cultus."* (2 Feb. 1974) http://w2.vatican.va/content/paul-vi/en/apost_exhortations/documents/hf_p-vi_exh_19740202_marialis-cultus.html.

Pelikan, Jaroslav. *Development of Christian Doctrine: Some Historical Prolegomena.* New Haven, CT: Yale University Press, 1969.

————. *Mary through the Centuries: Her Place in the History of Culture.* New Haven, CT: Yale University Press, 1996.

————. *The Vindication of Tradition: The 1983 Jefferson Lecture in the Humanities.* New Haven, CT: Yale University Press, 1984.

Pellauer, David, and Bernard Dauenhaurer. "Paul Ricoeur." In *Stanford Encyclopedia of Philosophy.* https://plato.stanford.edu/entries/ricoeur/.

Peterson, Eugene. *Eat This Book: A Conversation in the Art of Spiritual Reading.* Grand Rapids: Eerdmans, 2009.

Pidel, Aaron. "Ricoeur and Ratzinger on Biblical History and Hermeneutics." *Journal of Theological Interpretation* 8.2 (2014) 193–212.

Piguet, À Jean-Claude. "Detranscendentalizing Subjectivity: Paul Ricoeur's Revelatory Hermeneutics of Suspicion." http://www.geocities.ws/nythamar/ricoeur.html.

Bibliography

Pius IX. "December 8: The Immaculate Conception of the Blessed Virgin Mary: AV History and St. Anselm's Beautiful Sermon." Office of Readings. https://catholicsstrivingforholiness.com/2017/12/06/dec-8-the-immaculate-conception-of-the-blessed-virgin-mary-av-history-and-st-anselms-beautiful-sermon/.

———. *Ineffabilis Deus: The Immaculate Conception*. Papal Encyclicals Online. http://www.papalencyclicals.net/pius09/p9ineff.htm.

Pius XII. *Munificentissimus Deus*. National Catholic Welfare Conference. 1 Nov. 1950. http://w2.vatican.va/content/pius-xii/en/apost_constitutions/documents/hf_p-xii_apc_19501101_munificentissimus-deus.html.

Protoevangelium of James. New Advent. http://www.newadvent.org/fathers/0847.htm.

Rahner, Karl, SJ. *Theological Investigations*, Vol. I, translated by Cornelius Ernst, OP. 2nd ed. Abingdon, UK: Helicon, 1961.

Ratzinger, Joseph. *Daughter Zion*. San Francisco: Ignatius, 1983.

Read, Sally. "My Poetic Path to the Virgin." *Tablet*, 6 Apr. 2013.

Reynolds, Brian K. *Gateway to Heaven: Marian Doctrine and Devotion, Image and Typology in the Patristic and Medieval Periods*, Vol. 1: *Doctrine and Devotion (Theology and Faith)*. New York: New City, 2012.

Ricoeur, Paul. "Consent and Necessity." In *Freedom and Nature: The Voluntary and the Involuntary*, edited by John Wild. Evanston, IL: Northwestern University Press, 1966.

———. *Interpretation Theory: Discourse and the Surplus of Meaning*. Fort Worth, TX: Texas Christian University Press, 1976.

———. "The Summoned Subject in the School of the Narratives of the Prophetic Vocation." In *Figuring the Sacred: Religion, Narrative, and Imagination*, edited by Mark J. Wallace and translated by David Pellauer, 262–75. Minneapolis: Fortress, 1995.

———. *The Symbolism of Evil*. Boston: Beacon, 1967.

"R.I. Firefighter Seeks Help for Peers in Sarajevo." UPI. 22 Feb. 1993.

Ruether, Rosemary Radford. "Immaculate Conception of the Blessed Virgin Mary." In *A New Dictionary of Christian Theology*, edited by Alan Richardson and John Bowden. London: SCM, 1983.

———. *Mary: The Feminine Face of the Church*. Louisville, KY: Westminster John Knox, 1977.

Ryan, Jerry. "Orthodoxy & Dissent." *Commonweal*, 8 Feb. 2013.

Schneiders, Sandra Marie, IHM. "Faith, Hermeneutics, and the Literal Sense of Scripture." *Theological Studies* 39.4 (1978) 719–36.

Schroer, Silvia. *Wisdom Has Built Her House: Studies on the Figure of Sophia in the Bible*. Collegeville, MN: Liturgical, 2000.

Seaver, Patrick. "Our Lady: Second Person of the Blessed Trinity?!" *Furrow* 60.1 (2009) 44–47.

Shaw, Luci. "Annunciatory Angel." In *Accompanied by Angels: Poems of the Incarnation*. Grand Rapids: Eerdmans, 2006.

———. "Madonna and Child, with Saints." In *Accompanied by Angels: Poems of the Incarnation*. Grand Rapids: Eerdmans, 2006.

———. "The Overshadow, A Poem." https://www.outwalking.net/2006/12/the-overshadow.html.

Shea, John. "Two Prayers of Loss." In *The Hour of the Unexpected*. Allen, TX: Tabor, 1977.

Bibliography

Shoemaker, Stephen J. "Marian Liturgies and Devotion in Early Christianity." In *Mary: The Complete Resource*, edited by Sarah Jane Boss, 130–45. Oxford: Oxford University Press, 2007.

Shoemperlen, Diane. *Our Lady of the Lost and Found: A Novel of Mary, Faith, and Friendship*. New York: Viking, 2001.

Sisters of Mercy of the Americas. *Constitutions and Directory*. Silver Spring, MD, 1991, 2012.

Sisters of Mercy of the Union. *Constitutions of the Religious Sisters of Mercy of the Union in the United States of America*, 1955.

Sloyan, Gerard. "John." In *Interpretation: A Bible Commentary for Teaching and Preaching*. Louisville, KY: John Knox, 1988.

Smith, Zadie. *NW: A Novel*. New York: Penguin, 2012.

Spretnak, Charlene. *Missing Mary: The Queen of Heaven and Her Emergence in the Modern Church*. London: Palgrave Macmillan, 2004.

Steenberg, M. C. "Conceiving Jesus 'through the ear.'" Monachos.net. 19 Aug. 2003. http://www.monachos.net/conversation/topic/296-conceiving-jesus-through-the-ear/.

Stein, Edith. "Luxta Crucem Tecum Stare." Translated by Peter Heineff. In *Mary: Art, Culture, and Religion through the Ages*, edited by Caroline H. Ebertshauser et al., 117. New York: Crossroad, 1998.

Stone, Brian, ed. and trans. *Medieval English Verse*. Baltimore: Penguin, 1964.

Thompson, Thomas, ASM. "Vatican II and Beyond." In *Mary: A History of Doctrine and Devotion*, edited by Hilda Graef. Notre Dame: Ave Maria, 2009.

Thurian, Max. *Mary: Mother of All Christians*. New York: Herder & Herder, 1964.

Trible, Phyllis. "Love's Lyrics Redeemed." In *God and the Rhetoric of Sexuality: Overtures to Biblical Theology*, 144–65. Minneapolis: Fortress, 1978.

———. "A Love Story Gone Awry." In *God and the Rhetoric of Sexuality: Overtures to Biblical Theology*, 72–143. Minneapolis: Fortress, 1978.

Trouve, Marianne Lorraine, FSP, ed. "Dogmatic Constitution on the Church (*Lumen Gentium*), Chapter VIII." In *Mother of Christ, Mother of the Church: Documents on the Blessed Virgin Mary*. Boston: Daughters of St. Paul/Pauline, 2001.

Vanhoozer, Kevin J. *Is There a Meaning in This Text? The Bible, the Reader, and the Morality of Literary Knowledge*. 1999. Reprint, Nashville: Zondervan, 2009.

Vatican Council II. *The Documents of Vatican II*. Edited by Walter M. Abbott, SJ. Translated by Joseph Gallagher. New York: Herder and Herder, 1966.

Wakefield, Kathleen. "Mary's Poem." In *Divine Inspiration*. https://briarcroft.wordpress.com/tag/kathleen-wakefield/.

Ware, Kallistos. *The Orthodox Way*. Yonkers, NY: St. Vladimir's Seminary, 1995.

Warner, Marina. *Alone of All Her Sex: The Myth and the Cult of the Virgin Mary*. New York: Knopf, 1976.

Wells, Rebecca. *Divine Secrets of the Ya Ya Sisterhood*. New York: Harper Perennial, 2004.

Wellek, Rene. *A History of Modern Criticism: 1750–1950*. New Haven, CT: Yale University Press, 1955.

Williams, Rowan. "Weaving Scarlet and Purple: A Legend of Mary." In *Ponder These Things: Praying with Icons of the Virgin*. London: Sheed and Ward, 2002.

Winston-Allen, Anne. *Stories of the Rose: The Making of the Rosary in the Middle Ages*. University Park, PA: Pennsylvania State University Press, 1997.

Women in the Bible, eds. "Who Were Ruth and Naomi in the Bible?" http://www.womeninthebible.net/women-bible-old-new-testaments/ruth/.

Bibliography

Yeago, David S. "The Presence of Mary in the Mystery of the Church." In *Mary, Mother of God*, edited by Carl E. Braaten and Robert W. Jenson, 58–79. Grand Rapids: Eerdmans, 2004.

Yee, Gale A. *Poor Banished Children of Eve: Woman as Evil in the Hebrew Bible.* Minneapolis: Fortress, 2003.

Zimdars-Swartz, Sandra. *Encountering Mary: Visions of Mary from La Salette to Medjugorje.* New York: Avon, 1991.

Index of Subjects

Index of Names

Since this entire book is about Mary, the mother of Jesus, and about topics closely related to her, she is not personally listed in this Index of Names.

Made in the USA
Monee, IL
02 January 2024

50940366R00100